The Sifting Blade
OF THE MESSIAH
by Randy Shield

TABLE OF CONTENTS

THE PREFACE

"Our Reeling Planet"

2 Thessalonians 2

Concerning the coming of our Lord Jesus Christ and our being gathered to him, we ask you, brothers and sisters, not to become easily unsettled or alarmed by the teaching allegedly from us, whether by a prophecy or by word of mouth or by letter, asserting that the day of the Lord has already come. Don't let anyone deceive you in any way, for that day will not come until the rebellion occurs and the man of lawlessness revealed, the man doomed to destruction. He will oppose and will exalt himself over everything that is called God or is worshiped, so that he sets himself up in God's temple, proclaiming himself to be God.

"Truth is still the truth, even if no one believes it.
A lie is still a lie, even if everyone believes it."

After the exhaustion of writing the first two books of the Exodus Trilogy, the last thing I wanted was to write another book on prophecy. Yet this book is not just about prophecy, it is very different in content and intent. It is absolutely critical to this moment for the nation, for Israel and the prodigal church. Its focus is on the here and now, and why the ground is shaking beneath our feet. It is a mandate for deep change in the midst of the drowning deluge of darkness that is swallowing our planet, our nation, and our souls. What I am not looking forward to is the coming slander from those that are trapped in the shadowed theology that got us here.

This book is rooted in the sobering cries from reaching into hearts of incarcerated youth and adults in the clutches of desperation. My life for the last several decades has been spent on two severe missions. The first is having blood up to my elbows from the hearts of incarcerated kids. Secondly is an urgent warning to our perishing nation of the presiding apostate rebellion that Jesus warned us would come at the gate of the Tribulation. Our young people have not only been visited by the sins of their fathers, they have moved in. We now stand as an unrepentant nation as our children have embraced the same sinful ways as their own. In our nation, even many Christians have divorced the Bible as we pretend for the faith on Sunday, and we are fulfilling the warning from Christ of returning to the unrepentance in the Days of Noah.

If you are not truly seeking God for truth as why we have become a "nation of desperation," you might want to give this book to someone else. This is a trumpet call bathed in decades of searching the Bible for the truth, the whole truth and nothing but the truth. The prophet Jeremiah in lament asked, "Has a nation ever changed its gods? But my people have exchanged their glorious God for worthless idols." It is time to be alarmed and to be brutally honest where you stand before the Messiah. This is an overwhelming reality check to stop sowing among the thorns and get your eyes fixed on the Messiah and the harvest.

As Jesus sweat blood in the garden of Gethsemane, He fell to the ground and prayed that, if possible, the hour might pass from him. He prayed, "Abba Father, everything is possible for you. Take this cup from me. Yet not what I will, but your will be done." When he returned to his disciples and found them sleeping. He then went to the weary disciples saying, "Simon Peter, "Are you asleep? Couldn't you keep watch for one hour? Watch and pray so that you will not fall into temptation. The spirit is willing, but the flesh is weak."

My solemn prayer and hope for this book is to reach out to be a lifeline to the hungry seeking remnant without direction, to the believer trapped in unbelief trusting in the way of this age, and the starving unbeliever that is desperately looking for answers and hope as they are treading the waters of this present evil age. The cry to the harvesters is going out as the storm clouds are surrounding us. For centuries, God has patiently delayed His coming, giving humanity ample opportunity for repentance. But, as in the Days of Noah, His Spirit will not always strive with man. After the rapture of the faithful, His sifting judgment will be swift, relentless, and thorough. His sharp sickle will leave every indicted person without excuse, just as a sickle swung into a harvest of wheat leaves no stalk standing. If you truly asking, "Where does this leave me?" Then this book is for you.

CHAPTER ONE

The Sifting Journey into the Valley of Decision

Matthew 24

Jesus left the temple and was walking away when his disciples came up to him to call his attention to its buildings. "Do you see all these things?" he asked. "Truly I tell you, not one stone here will be left on another; everyone will be thrown down. As Jesus was sitting on the Mount of Olives, the disciples came to him privately. "Tell us, "They said, "when will this happen, and what will be the sign of your coming and of the end of the age?"

"Suddenly summoned to witness something great and horrendous, we keep fighting not to reduce it to our own smallness." John Updike

As a very young man, I was fascinated over the moment of our journey to the moon as Neil Armstrong spoke the famous quote, "One small step for man, one giant leap for mankind." This is where I realized the explosive power of technology that was spoken from the Book of Daniel. Years later, I was able to visit Cape Canaveral in Florida where they house the rocket and the space capsule in separate buildings. I was absolutely astonished by both vehicles. Compared to the technology of today the interior of the capsule was absolutely primitive and miniscule. It seemed impossible that the astronauts could have survived; their courage must have been immeasurable.

In comparison, the size of the Apollo rocket in its massive warehouse is impossible to describe. Envisioning being strapped in that tiny primitive capsule on top of this mountain of fuel is something I cannot begin to imagine. The first stage of the rocket alone, carried 1,400,000 pounds of fuel. This amazing journey to the moon is a vague parable of the treacherous journey we face stepping forward into the colossal Day of Evil. This brings into perspective the small step from our personal life to the massive and giant leap we have taken into the oppressive, godless global culture.

The two hinge pins of purpose that this final generation are swinging upon are the sifting of Israel and the transforming remnant being separated within the nominal church. The present giant collage of the ten-horned Bestial Empire and the Mysterious Harlot are the dark canvas they are appearing as these overcomers are arising. This substantiates why so many are awakening as we are about to enter the gates of the volatile Tribulation.

In a former book, "The Book of Revelation at Ground Zero, I shared that to understand this revelation, you must envision it from the audience of an ancient Greek play with the actors on a moving stage with a reeling timeline. Faithfulness, courage, and integrity are woven within the lives of the heartful players, as the majority are full of violence, corruption, and deceit. The mission of the Book of Revelation is a grave warning to take it to heart as the sifting occurs.

To begin the Book of Revelation, the Apostle John falls dead at Christ's feet, paralyzed from reverential fear, because of the majesty of the Messiah's appearing. John had accepted the first vein of prophecy concerning the Messiah before his eyes earlier, but this was far beyond his comprehension. The fire from His eyes and His feet would soon try the works and the heart of man through righteousness. The most alarming thing was the two-edged sword protruding from His mouth. Perhaps it was having to connect the dots between the mercy and the righteous judgment of Christ that was so hard to bear. Yet, the anchor to John's heart was that he was the one that Jesus loved and was the one that laid his head upon Jesus' breast. The two-edged sword from His mouth is first represented in the Book of Hebrews where His Word is living and surgical, even to the dividing of soul and spirit. It is now doing its sifting work in the souls of men preparing them for the great harvest. This sword finally appears in the Valley of Decision from His mouth, sifting the global armies before Israel.

We will now investigate the crucial pieces of the puzzle that the Messiah is sifting before the coming hour of trial we are facing. The tremors are touching each of our lives in so many ways. After the chiseling of Peter, he warned, "Dear friends, do not be surprised at the fiery ordeal that has come upon you to test you, as though something strange were happening to you. As we reach the final chapter of the church age, we must learn again to fight on our knees.

Outcast from Eden

Genesis 2

The LORD God took the man and put him in the Garden of Eden to work it and take care of it. And the LORD God commanded the man, "You are free to eat from any tree in the garden; but you must not eat from the tree of the knowledge of good and evil, for when you eat from it you will certainly die." The LORD God said, "It is not good for the man to be alone. I will make a helper suitable for him."

In the heart of God's beautiful creation was placed the "apple of His eye." Nothing was kept from them save the certainty that it would be eternal; and at this point they felt no fear. Adam and Eve had no idea of a previous realm stained by the evil of betrayal that had broken the Lord's heart. As they danced in the flowers of grace . they had no understanding that above them swarmed fallen angels and the disembodied spirits of those who had rebelled against the Most High. Tragically, they were destined to be overwhelmed by evil and deception to experience the tragic word, death. They would feel the terror of His wrath, and the horrors of corruption by the evilest predator.

The Lord already knew the great obstacle to perfection from His earlier created being and that until this great flaw of sin could be removed, He was unable to show full measure of His love. He could not bestow humanity men with greater power and wisdom, until they had passed the danger of abusing His grace, and so falling as the sinful angels had done before them.

A greater fall then came in the tenth generation from Adam to Noah's generation as God's forbearance held back judgment in the hope that mankind would come to repentance. The Days of Noah shed a total rebellion against God's ways and would be seeded in the Way of Cain. Cain's perverted cauldron of selfishness and delusion was poured out on that time upon his followers, and his conspiracy with the fallen angels began to consume the earth. After the seduction in the garden, it brought a full-fledged invasion by Satan, the Prince of this World, and his conspiring myriad of fallen Watchers. This had left the globe in a spiritual eclipse beyond the pale of darkness. This was the twisted campaign from the first angelic rebellion with its invasion to thwart God's new creation and to hijack it into his delusive submission.

The perpetual journey from Eden into the wilderness experience changed the relationship of God with humanity. In the Garden of Eden, everything was provided for Adam and Eve. It was a protected place, where they had no worry or fear. All they had to do was tend the garden, enjoy its benefits and protect it. After the deluge, everything changed to covenant with mankind through the rainbow for the redemptive process through the wilderness experience. From Genesis forward, God enters into one formal relationship after another by disciplinary covenant to rescue man from himself and the prince of darkness.

The process of sifting was introduced in the wilderness or plains between a brazen hunter and an idol worshipper. The hearts of both Nimrod and Abraham could not have been more different, yet their heritage was the same. Nimrod sought a name for himself reaching to the stars for godhood. Abraham reached for God and redemption through coming out to the place that the Lord would show him. This will lead us through many covenants and many pieces to the puzzle to find our redemption through the mysterious Messiah. It will answer what Jesus meant when he testified, "For many are invited, but few are chosen."

The Puzzling Piece of Israel

I speak the truth in Christ, I am not lying, my conscience confirms it through the Holy Spirit, have great sorrow and unceasing anguish in my heart. For I could wish that I myself were cursed and cut off from Christ for the sake of my people, those of my own race, the people of Israel. Theirs is the adoption to sonship; theirs the divine glory, the covenants, the receiving of the law, the temple worship and the promises. Theirs are the patriarchs, and from them is traced the human ancestry of the Messiah, who is God over all, forever praised.

"True liberty consists exactly in self-determination in the direction of holiness. Man is never freer than when he moves consciously in the direction of God." Louis Berkhof

The promise of the Messiah was birthed through Eve's fall to sin, creating the desperate need for a Savior. From the promise of the Messiah's redemption. His veins would begin to flow as Abraham stepped out from the wilderness of the Chaldees. As the present evil age continues the despisal of Abraham's seed, Israel is still a mystery to the unbelieving world. The perception of the nation of Israel even among Christians is confused and distorted in many ways.

The covenant with Israel continued with Moses and contained the foundations of the written Torah and the Lord's purpose. In this covenant, God makes it clear that Israel is His treasured possession upon the earth and His foundation for restoration as a " kingdom of priests and a holy nation," if they follow His commandments with sacrifice. Beyond its central spiritual purpose, the Mosaic covenant was also political. Israel was established as a theocracy to mirror the kingdom of heaven with the rule of law to the globe.

The kingdom of Israel suffered and fell continually, because they just couldn't be monogamous to their Lord. Their continual affairs with settled rebellion eventually brought four hundred years of silence from the Lord. They were carnally distorted and would eventually would go into a final exile after rejecting their Messiah. They were "ever learning, but never able to come to the knowledge of the truth.

The only thing more mystifying than this nation was the appearance of their awaited Messiah, who they rejected as a threat. Jesus never came to destroy the way of the law and the prophets. He came to fulfill it. He came to the Jewish first, but most of them not only misunderstood Him; they rejected Him. There has been a wall of partition ever since with a fault line from the cross that has separated the called. Christ's purpose in the cross was to make both Jew and Gentile one new man in the Messiah. He made it possible for Jew and Gentile to be brothers by fulfilling the law so that we could witness through the Messiah as one. Even today, this has been sifted by sibling rivalry and ignorance.

We now live in a sobering moment in history as the assault upon Israel is at epic proportion. As believers in Jesus Christ, we are to take a stand for Israel. This is one thing that has shielded us from being cursed as a nation, yet sadly we are wavering. This is not to be based on politics, distorted religious ideology, but the vision and determination from the heart of the Bible. The Word of God declares there will come a time when all the nations of the world will turn against Israel. This imminent prophecy of a final persecution has already catalyzed in the Middle East as the epicenter consuming the planet. Few truly understand that Jerusalem is the "apple of His eye."

I have a God-given love for Israel as I do for our nation, yet I feel completely devastated from the continual "unbelief," and the self-determination of both nations. I would be remiss to not mention the torrential persecution that Israel is facing right now is quickly turning upon the church from a multifaceted global regime. The tsunami of antisemitism has flooded every shore on the earth. In my worst nightmare, I could never imagine that something worse would happen to Israel that could overshadow the holocaust of the Third Reich.

This new wave of deception and unscriptural perception flows through the apostate media like "a river to the sea," but the Lord will be the One to set the final boundaries. Ironically, Abraham, Israel's father of faith, became the first authentic "Hebrew," which means "river crosser." How ironic this term is as the world cries out their devilish mantra, "from the river to the sea." I pray daily for this chosen nation from a heavy heart as we witness the rise of the "Fourth Reich." which is provoking the systematic godlessness, "selfism," and a blindness to every principle and code in the scripture. Please be at peace we will see the rest of the story as the wind begins to blow.

The Puzzling Piece of the Church

Acts 1

He said to them: "It is not for you to know the times or dates the Father has set by his own authority. But you will receive power when the Holy Spirit comes on you; and you will be my witnesses in Jerusalem, and in all Judea and Samaria, and to the ends of the earth." After he said this, he was taken up before their very eyes, and a cloud hid him from their sight.

"Contemporary people tend to examine the Bible, looking for things they can't accept; but Christians should reverse that, allowing the Bible to examine us, looking for things God can't accept." Timothy Keller

The church age brought forth the eternal vision for God's plan to include the Gentiles, but not at the expense of His first covenant with Israel. Since the first century, salvation comes uniquely through faith in Jesus the Messiah with its beginning exclusively to Israel. God's purpose for the Jewish people still remains unchanged, despite the majority have rejected their Messiah. Yet, there has always been a faithful remnant and in the future, there will be a widespread turning by Jews to faith in their Messiah.

The church has always faced tempering from persecution to seduction just like Israel. From the very beginning, Israel's fatigue led them to apathy, as compromise led to comfort, that eventually led to their exile. Revival had been essential from fatigue setting in from a lack of fresh fire. Revival is restoration through God's presence to His people and it will complete us if we will repent and return to our first love.

Even more puzzling than Israel is the perplexing church age, especially at its compromising conclusion. When we look at church history, the Prince of this World has employed his only two tactics of persecution and seductive embracement to distort and fragment her testimony. Satan is now feverishly sifting Christians by persecuting the faithful and indulging the nominal apostate. In his foolishness as he did at Calvary, he is helping to complete the will of God, not crucify it. This twisting serpent will soon realize the cry from our Messiah that "It is finished."

As the first church deployed, they were forced to live and breathe together clinging to life and to the Spirit of Christ. This produced great beauty and a fervent witness that was manifested in the final history of the disciples. They were all martyred except for John who lived through being boiled in oil. There is a polarizing testimony of the church in history. She has either glowed in the flames from her deep suffering and conviction, or has been impaled by compromise and apostasy as Israel. There is no doubt that the prince of this world is employing both to separate the nominal from the remnant. As he did at the cross, he is completing the will of God, not defeating it.

The confusion has come from misunderstanding the heart of the beginning. In the garden of Gethsemane in the Valley of Kidron, Jesus was deeply distraught at the spiritual horror waiting for Him on the cross. He would take our place as a guilty sinner and receive all the spiritual punishment that we deserve. The battle of His cross was first won with prayer and the sweating blood in a garden that was far from the paradise of Eden. The called remnant of disciples began to take the same steps of their forefather, Israel, by repeating their boasting in a crossless endeavor. What is at stake today is the same cross Peter said he would bare, but refused it. Yet, Jesus knew Peter would fail, but Jesus wouldn't forsake him but walk him through his own valley of decision.

An even greater betrayal awaited Jesus as Judas betrayed Him "with a kiss." Jesus knew the heart of Judas had been filled by the evil one. Jesus could have fled, escaping the agony waiting for Him at the cross, but Jesus rose to meet Judas directly. This night, the great eternal sifting began its journey from the Valley of Kidron to the inevitable Valley of Decision. The gate of the church is the cross that would have to be embraced by His followers. But as Israel the travel was treacherous, self-determination would continue until the vessel was broken at Pentecost.

The love and peace in the first church age of the Book of Acts was immeasurable in the midst of severe tribulation. From the outside, no one dared to join the church without the revelation of the cost. Its fellowship was a very dangerous place to be, as they concealed in catacombs and caves. **Yet, as the fear was quenched, the signs and wonders inflamed** the true Word of God where the Spirit of God exploded in glory. Then Satan with his first weapon of persecution scattered the church from Jerusalem in vain, for the eternal seeds were already planted.

As the church began to distance itself from Judaism, rivalry and tribalism began to divide the church. Even Paul wrestled with Peter over the issue of how the Old Covenant interfacing with the New Covenant. At first. Paul had to defend the gospel against the heresy of the so-called "Judaizers" continued the lie of self-justification as Peter relented under pressure and separated himself from the church in Antioch, yet a new heresy surfaced from the opposite perception.

This current debate continues which maintains an opposite view over whether God has replaced Israel with the church. The lingering doctrine of "replacement theology" is the idea that the church has completely replaced Israel. **The crisis of rejecting the first covenant of Israel through errant teaching has continued for centuries. This fatal mistake is like building without a foundation, and it negates the validity of the thorough prophecies even occurring at this moment.**

Without the true eternal revelation of repentance and devotion, we are locked out where there can be no redemption. We must remember the past and learn from it, as God is sovereignly bringing the Jews to a new awakening, He is also trying to awaken the church from its slumber. As the four hundred years of silence were finally broken through John the Baptist, the silence again is about to be broken. As Jesus Christ, our Messiah lifts His hand from the prodigal church through the rapture she will be exposed for who she is. The nominal church must repent from being an enterprise, and find its way its way back to the beginning.

We desperately need a "new awakening" from the slumber to repent. Repentance does not eliminate the struggle with sin and make us perfect immediately. If we turn from apathy, we will cease from lawlessness of this present evil age. The truth is that only a remnant will pay the price to abandon this present evil age. **We must ask the question, "are we betraying Him with a kiss?" Now is the time for your decision.**

The Descent of Our Nation

"When I shut up the heavens so that there is no rain, or command locusts to devour the land or send a plague among my people, if my people, who are called by my name, will humble themselves and pray and seek my face and turn from their wicked ways, then I will hear from heaven, and I will forgive their sin and will heal their land.

"We are not diplomats but prophets, and our message is not a compromise but an ultimatum." A.W. Tozer

A simple search on the topic of character and leadership yielded thousands of books and quotes from history, but the Word of God is what sustains us. Character is so important that Paul recognized it as a principal requirement of faith. and an essential prerequisite for all relationships. National character is just as critical, yet we have drifted into a post-Christian nation. As we left the apostasy of the past overseas, we are slowly realizing that it has not left us. I now will ask what is the source of our national identity today? What is shaping our character and do we live as witnesses to the Lord? Sadly, the leaven that has crept in from our inception is now "leavening the whole lump."

Our nation once stood strong in faith until the fracture of slavery appeared that crossed the ocean from Europe with us was finally confronted. This first fracture brought division that began our own slow motion sifting. Next, the Industrial Revolution was imported and changed the culture from the farms to the cities germinating the loss of innocence to indulgence. The "Roaring Twenties" enticed the first moral collapse.

When the Great Depression crashed the economy, it terminated the slide into the obsession with greed and materialism. The next great shaking came with World War Two. Pearl Harbor shocked us and forced us out of hiding. This turned the tide of the war with an enormous price to the nation. World War Two awakened our national character as we stood against the Third Reich that was swallowing Europe and annihilating Israel.

After licking our wounds from the war, we began to hide in media, new technology, and returned to the idol of materialism during the "Fifties." The "Sixties" became the crisis point of no return when we began to forget God as we began worshipping at the altar of "selfism." This began our complete descent into our own Diaspora, fragmenting us from the brutal Mystery of Lawlessness. This brought the warning from Jesus that would impale us on the love of most growing cold destroying our families, our culture and even many of our churches. Our descent has now led us downward step by step, generation by generation to the doorway of betraying "Generation Z" from the spiritual facelift that has made us unrecognizable. My heart breaks for what they have inherited.

God's template for the nations that rebel against Him is now being applied to us as it was in the silent years before John the Baptist. We have become a pagan nation worshiping at the altar of sensuality, and greed. Fredrich Tietze, a German author from the godless post-modern era was responsible for the old saying, "the devil is in the details," yet it could never be more truthful, than in this deadly scheme of the evil one.

As the Lord Himself put the words of warning in the prophet Jeremiah's mouth to "Sow righteousness for yourselves and reap faithful love; break up your unplowed ground and stop sowing amongst the thorns. It is time to seek the LORD until he comes and sends righteousness on you like the rain." This is a parable for the general character and contradiction of our nation. We are not only mocking God; we are imitating previous nations by rejecting every facet of the faith. As Rome, we are worshipping the creation rather than the Creator to the point that we even are denying God's existence. The true "climate change" is the spiritual perversion and conversion to rebellion.

We are now experiencing the returning hand of the coming reaper with His blade of righteousness. The time for humbling and sifting has come, either within or without. As Israel, we have been carried off into exile not by foreigners but by the work of our own hands. Refusing His hand, we have been warned not to put off the coming "Day of Evil" as we dance around the golden calf that Israel did. He is compelling us to come out and stand in the Light. I pray daily for this chosen nation from a heavy heart as we witness the rise of the "Fourth Reich" overseas. As the Prince of this World weaves his web of the Mystery of Lawlessness, it is provoking the systematic godlessness, "selfism," and a blindness to every principle and command in the scripture. This is a moral collapse that has not existed since the days of Noah and Sodom. The silence of the Gospel is blaring in the prodigal church as it is exchanged for acceptance from a nation gone mad.

The Descent of the Nations

1 John 5

And we know that the Son of God has come to this world, and has given us understanding and insight so that we may progressively and personally know Him who is true; and we are in Him who is true, in His Son Jesus Christ. We know that we are of God, and the whole world around us is encircled by the power of the evil one opposing God and His precepts. AMP

The Apostle John indicted Satan as the author of confusion. He exposed his scheme by amplifying, "We know that we are of God, and the whole world around us is encircled by the power of the evil one opposing God and His precepts." As a sorcerer encircles a pentagram over his prey, Satan is invoking his manipulation and control through a sorcerous cauldron of darkness over planet earth.

The Greek word, "cosmos" means "systematized error" which is the web of evil devised by Satan in opposition to God and His called people. It is the course of this age streaming confusion through the final fallen conglomerate empire, and their falling kings. Error can be divided into two components: random error and systematic error. Systematic error is not determined by circumstance, but it is introduced by an intended conspirator causing havoc through the convergence. The Prince of this World's invaded our planet with evil deception in the Garden of Eden by shifting the focus from God to what can be termed the greater deceptive mission of "selfism."

This generation has been systematized through villains and villainous systems. Since the last world war, the evil one has contrived a web of deceit stand by strand as God's way and His Word has been neglected or rejected as we repeat the rebellion in Noah's day. It revolves around technology, media, sorcerous religion and a contrived economics. Its taskmasters are centered in the United Nations, through corrupt politicians in Washington D. C, in Europe and through global financiers veiled in secrecy. The described "deep state" has gone global. This deep state is a type of governance made up of potentially secret and unauthorized networks of power operating independently of the state's political leadership in pursuit of their own agenda and goals. They dwell among us betraying God and the nation.

The final stage of the statue of Nebuchadnezzar exposed by the prophet Daniel is this presiding "New World Order" we have been warned about since the seditious Nazis almost completed the task. The traitors in our midst now conspire with the United Nations and many tentacles to bring the nations under the framework of globalization. It is even coercing our nation to subside into its iron and clay venue of socialistic domination through the veiled intimidation of power.

The present fifth and final kingdom that Daniel warned us is set apart in time from the others as it appears as the revival of the Roman Empire right before eyes as the harlot global media spreads its lies and propaganda on through the worldwide web. Daniel was able to reveal the consecutive four thousand years of world domination to the present from a single dream. The detail and the description through composites give us a distinct vision into the horizontal war plan of God's enemy. This dream gave us the understanding that this last empire will be crushed, as Christ, the Rock of ages returns. If this confuses you it is because Satan is the author of confusion.

The Encroaching New Dark Age

2 Thessalonian 2

But mark this: There will be terrible times in the last days. People will be lovers of themselves, lovers of money, boastful, proud, abusive, disobedient to their parents, ungrateful, unholy, without love, unforgiving, slanderous, without self-control, brutal, not lovers of the good, treacherous, rash, conceited, lovers of pleasure rather than lovers of God, having a form of godliness but denying its power. Have nothing to do with such people.

General Norman Schwarzkoph appeared in the Iraqi War in the year of 2003. He was the leader of the coalition of nations to lead the war against Iraq and Saddam Hussein. He **was** nicknamed **"Stormin' Norman"** for his fiery temper and his keen strategic mind. As he led the coalition into Iraq, he summarized the basic tactic of warfare in dismembering an enemy. **Schwarzkopf defined that you first behead your enemy which is to cut off the head from the body.** This first tactic to cut off the head of the enemy led to dismembering an enemy piece by piece, severing any type communication.

The Apostle Paul warned us to not be ignorant of the schemes of the devil, especially in war. Our Pledge of Allegiance was founded on the proclamation, "one nation under God, indivisible with liberty and justice for all." The first ploy of the enemy toward our nation was to sever our culture from relationship with God. A fatal blow that I witnessed as a youngster was the removal of prayer from school and then the government. The cutting off of the head led to removing the heart. The worst in school used to be smoking in the restroom to skipping class. Now we have resorted to Uzis with mass shootings being a norm.

Secondly, the fall of our nation from being "indivisible" came as the cancer of "tribalism." It disemboweled our nation from its origin as it activated the Mystery of lawlessness. Tribalism is the state of an existing tribe in rabid unity and loyalty to an order of the political, or race, or gender, or of gangs so that it sifts you from all others. The most bewildering order is the guillotine of a "cancel culture" has created a cultic dissolution even within the family structure. It is addition through subtraction.

It is imperative that we also understand the definition for culture. It is "a system of learned and shared beliefs, language, norms, and values that a group uses to identify themselves and provide a framework within which to live and work." Like technology, this is not inherently evil, unless it became a form of ungodliness. The immersing contamination in the systematized global culture is blatant, but you may be asking, "what has this have to do with me?" Absolutely everything.

Satan has refined this scheme through the centuries and he now has deployed it through the sorcery of "selfism." The enemy has especially conspired to separate the body of Christ through severing the Word of God and His Holy Spirit. Tragically, there are over forty-five thousand denominations (divisions) in Christianity. Satan has flooded the earth and divided humanity through every form of Tribalism. This is the first step in inciting warfare. Sadly, at this point liberty and justice has left the building as the blade of the Messiah is visiting in tune, separating the wheat from the chaff.

Here is a song that I was inspired to write on this global collusion.

The Web
The day of destruction is drawing so near
His voice of deception has calmed all your fears
A thread from the power
A thread from the gold
A thread of desire has driven your soul
Into the web of the reaper
Into the dark of the night
In his web of delusion, he will squeeze out your life

The day of salvation is drawing so near
His voice of redemption has dried all your tears
A thread from the power
A thread from the gold
A thread of repentance has driven your soul
Into the net of salvation
Into the heart of the light
In his net of refining, he will sift out your life

FINDING THE
LORD MESSIAH

CHAPTER TWO

Understanding Our Mysterious Messiah

Isaiah 53

He was despised and rejected by mankind,

a man of suffering, and familiar with pain.

Like one from whom people hide their faces

he was despised, and we held him in low esteem.

Surely, he took up our pain

and bore our suffering,

yet we considered him punished by God,

stricken by him, and afflicted.

But he was pierced for our transgressions,

he was crushed for our iniquities;

the punishment that brought us peace was on him,

and by his wounds we are healed.

"The only way to find the meaning and purpose of your life is to find it in a mystery, the mystery of Him, and to make that mystery the cause of everything you do and the reason for everything you are."
Jonathan Cahn

The incredible Word of God is the Book of Life written in the blood of the Messiah flowing in promise from Genesis through the Book of Revelation. He is the mediator between God and man, the Old Covenant and the New Covenant in the Spirit of prophecy. The manifestation of the Spirit of prophecy builds through all of the dispensations from the first Adam to the second Adam's Messianic triumphant return. As we validated the fatal fall of Adam and Eve that brought forth the desperate need for a Messiah; sinfulness had initiated death intoxicating humanity. As the gates of Eden were closed by the angels, the family of Adam was exiled, being sifted from an intimate relationship with their Creator. This provoked the yearning prophecy for the Deliverer to restore the intimacy that was lost. This road of peril has been traveled by the seed of Abraham, especially from the Diaspora to this very day.

The loss of an eternal connection with the Lord provoked the hopelessness of Israel through the ages. Since the birth of Christ, the Jewish culture has been walking around the cross for centuries, refusing to look into the face of their Redeemer. The dilemma of the mystery of the Messiah is far more than just the meaning of the cross; it is the meaning of life. As nominal, professing Christians are repeating walking around the cross, they also are refusing the King of glory and His Lordship as Israel.

The word for Messiah, "mashiach" means "the Anointed One," the expected Deliverer and King. The Greek translation of Messiah is "Christos" meaning "the Christ." To the Israelites, the Messiah was referred to as the coming king that God promised would defeat the evil world order surrounding them and bring hope and holiness back to the earth. Israel had been looking for their Messiah king from their beginning, until they decided they wanted a king to sooth their worldly woes and desires, one that resembled a worldly king.

Messianic prophecy is the heartbeat from the beginning to the end of Biblical prophecy. There is no way to express how important it is to have the revelation of the eternal way that streams throughout the scripture. The inspired prophets spoke with one voice for the repentance of Israel, to return and find the way to the Messiah. Jesus boldly declared, "I am the way, the truth, and the life. No one comes to the Father except through me." This was a stumbling block to Israel and today it has become a stumbling block to the prodigal church from ignoring the validity of the Word of God as the true King.

The prophets had prophesied Jesus was to be born into a poor family, with no known physical father, never to be crowned king of Israel until the end, but in deference received a crown of thorns, and was crucified by the Romans at their demand. While these expectations were raised, most of the nation failed to grasp the full role of the Messiah. They failed to grasp the expectations in the prophetic writings from the prophet Isaiah and others that the Messiah would not only be a political ruler but also a Divine suffering servant in the Father.

Tracing the historic journey of Israel is a tragic story of a broken relationship going through centuries "of ever learning but never coming to the knowledge of the truth." In the time of the second Temple, before its destruction, this Messianic hope returned and began to flourish. Later, the Jewish people continued to look for a king and political Messiah who would deliver them from the iron heel of Roman occupation and oppression. It was during this time that Jesus Christ arrived, but according to their perception of Jewish teaching, He did not fit their description of the promised Messiah. They missed the mark in expecting a royal earthly leader already established.

This generation was bombarded with the truth of Christ the Messiah. They should also have known from the prophet Zechariah that the Messiah would not come to Jerusalem as a mighty conquering king, but that he would come in peace, humility and gentleness, riding upon a donkey. The Book of Daniel further revealed that he would not immediately overthrow the oppressive gentile Kingdoms, but would establish the kingdom of God in the midst of them.

Judaism had constantly reinterpreted the Messianic hope. Instead of looking first for a "personal Messiah" healing their wounds, they look for a "Messianic Age" that brings forth a humanist king to compel world leaders with negotiating peace. They believe universal peace, righteousness, and justice will establish a new world order where Israel will enjoy peace in her land forever. This is tragically the coming entrapment of the Antichrist. Throughout their long history the Jewish people have renewed the messianic hope during times of persecution and suffering, but that hope dims with apathy when they live in peace and security. Right now, this history is repeating as the cry for their extinction is upon them, this will be the hook set in their mouth as the final worldly king comes with his promise of "peace and security. They will soon be seduced by a deceptive king, not only with feet of clay, but with the heart of Satan.

Jesus is truly the Savior, but He is also the Lord. During the prophetic period of Israel's history, the Jewish people were promised that God would raise up a redeemer from the seed of David who would bring the physical deliverance from their Gentile enemies, restore the Temple, and reestablish the kingdom rule of David. The dilemma was that they refused to recognize the Divine Savior from the Father, because they refused to acknowledge the sin that was their true oppressor, not the nations. There wind of the Messianic hope is beginning to blow through the house of Israel.

The Two Prophetic Veins of the Promised Messiah

Zechariah 12

"Then I will pour out a spirit of grace and prayer on the family of David and on the people of Jerusalem. They will look on me whom they have pierced and mourn for him as for an only son. They will grieve bitterly for him as for a firstborn son who has died.

All of the Father's eternal plan is filled with grace, investing in His Son and the work of the cross. Moses brought this revelation through the Law to Israel, but it never took root. The law was given to Israel to help them understand that they could never measure up on their own. It would only be in the Messiah that the power of their flesh could be eradicated and God's authority come in the person of the Holy Spirit as the Comforter.

The Scriptures speak of two distinct veins of prophecy concerning the Messiah. The first is His entrance as a humble servant destined to suffer and die for His people, He was to cleanse His people to be as white as snow. In the ancient Middle Eastern world, leaders rode horses if they rode to war, but donkeys if they came in peace. Jesus came on a donkey, symbolizing a new way for peace that they had never experienced. The prophet Zechariah understood what was to be revealed through the Messiah. "If we are worthy, the Messiah will come in the clouds. But if we are unworthy, he will come riding on a donkey." This reveals how out of order and reversed Israel is concerning their Messiah. This stumbling continues until it gets resolved. Until that happens, we cannot expect their King.

The prophecies about the Messiah are an incredibly intricate collection of predictions randomly placed throughout the Old Testament, and then fulfilled in the New Testament. It is an incredible mosaic of the all-inclusive Christ. They form one unified promise of God that split into two different veins and two different dispensations. We need to continually pray for the peace of Jerusalem and that Israel turns their heart back to their Messiah.

The Detailed Prophetic Scripture of the Messiah

John 21

Jesus did many other things as well. If every one of them were written down, I suppose that even the whole world would not have room for the books that would be written. Jesus did many other things as well. If every one of them were written down, I suppose that even the whole world would not have room for the books that would be written.

There are over three hundred prophecies in the Old Testament regarding the Messiah. Almost all were predicted hundreds and thousands of years before. At some times in Israel's history, the anticipation of Messiah's coming was great, while at other times the sense of expectancy waned. An example was the Messianic expectations in first-century Palestine at the Christ's first coming were heightened from the occupation by the Roman empire.

Jewish tradition revealed many things about their coming Messiah. First, He would be an offshoot of their favored King David. He will gather them from the four corners of the earth and restore the consecrated Torah Law covering the earth bringing peace to the globe. This consummation came from the prophet Isaiah in a vision of the coming millennium where the wolf will dwell with the lamb and the calf with the lion. The Messiah will restore the Edenic age of paradise.

I remember years ago, coincidentally meeting a passionate Messianic Jew who was an Israeli jet pilot in their air force. He excitedly told me that he had dreams of being in his plane over Megiddo as the Messiah parted the sky at His return. We must pray that this kind of passion soon returns to all of Israel as they ready to receive their King. Except for a remnant, the continuing concern of Israel over their surrounding enemies overwhelms them today as they refuse to look up for the salvation from their Messiah. The Jewish belief in the Messiah must understand the two advents. Most still reject Christ as their Messiah looking only to the future. Part of this is they did not understand his first coming as a perfect Lamb of sacrifice and then He would return to usher in world peace at their rescue in the Valley of Decision. It is critical that we not only pray for the peace of Jerusalem, but that we reach out with the Gospel of peace as the wind of antisemitism is raging again. They need a full revelation of the Lord Jesus Christ and turn to Him in this brutal time of trial.

Prophecies on the Heritage of the Messiah

- **The First Messianic Prophecy**
  This concerned the enmity between Eve through the cunning serpent. God promised that eventually the serpent would bruise the heel of the seed of the woman, but the Messiah would crush his head. (Genesis 3)
- **The Seed of Abraham**
  He would descend from the seed of Abraham to bless all of the nations on earth. (Genesis 12).
- **His Divinity**
  He was be born of a virgin, and they shall call His name Immanuel, undeniably meaning "God with us." (Isaiah 7)
- **His Birth**
  He would be born in Bethlehem of Judah. (Micah 5)
- **His Declaration**
  He rode into Jerusalem on a donkey as the righteous Savior coming with gentleness. (Zechariah 9)

The heart and soul of our Messiah's first coming was rooted in suffering to redeem humanity from their carnal will. The prophet Isaiah defined Him as the "man of sorrows." It is mesmerizing how Jesus walked through death and came to redeeming the repentant lost. But the Book of Hebrews explicitly tells us that He learned obedience through the things that he suffered. Mysteriously, it perfected Him as the source of eternal salvation for those who receive and obey Him.

Prophecies on the Suffering Messiah in the Old Testament.

- **The Deliverer**
  The Messiah would be the seed of a woman and would crush the head of Satan. (Genesis 3).
- **The Savior**
  He would be pierced for our transgression and crushed for our iniquities. (Isaiah 53).
- **His Death**
  He would die among the wicked ones but be buried with the rich. (Isaiah 53).
- **Forsaken**
  He will be forsaken even by His disciples. (Zechariah 13).
- **Ridiculed**
  The Messiah will be mocked, beaten and spit upon.
  (Isaiah 50)
- **His Clothing Sold**
  They cast lots for His clothes. (Psalm 22)
- **The Ransom Payment**
  The Messiah will be sold for thirty pieces of silver purchasing a potter's field. (Zechariah 11)
- **Hung on a tree**
  They would be hung from the poll of a tree.
  (Deuteronomy 21)
- **He Dies with Sinners**
  The Messiah will be crucified with criminals. (Isaiah 53)
- **Crucified**
  The Messiah will be pierced through His hands and feet. (Psalm 22)
- **Refuses Treatment**
  The Messiah will be given vinegar and gall to drink.
  (Psalm 69)

As the vision of the Messiah increased throughout the course of the Old Testament, the prophets gave more messages that the Messiah's origin is of God. Many of the prophecies don't specifically use the word "Messiah," though they came to be understood referenced to a future human deliverer. They believed the Messiah's only purpose was to bring about the return of the Jews from exile, to raise a higher level of devotion and love, and to reinstate the Jewish kingdom originally under King David. Sadly, this carnal perspective was not based from the eternal truth.

Prophecies about the Messianic King in the Old Testament

- **His Eternal Throne**
  He would have a throne, a kingdom and a dynasty
  starting with King David. (2 Samuel 7)
- **He was God**
  He would be called "Wonderful Counselor," "Mighty God,"
  (Isaiah 9)
- **The Newborn King**
  "Where is the newborn king of the Jews? We saw his star as
  it rose, and we have come to worship him."
  (Matthew 2)
- **The Humble King**
  The humility of Christ is displayed as He enters Jerusalem to
  fulfil His place as Messiah. "See, your king comes to you,
  righteous and victorious, lowly and riding on a donkey, on a
  colt, the foal of a donkey." (Zechariah 9)

So many today believe the return of Jesus Christ to the earth as the Messiah is the coming rapture, but this is His redeeming the faithful remnant for celebration of the wedding feast. His actual return will be after the church age as the mantle of the kingdom is handed to the 144,000 witnesses of Israel. The final piece of the puzzle for Israel will come as Israel's Messiah parts the skies on His white horse and splits the Mount of Olives to shield the Messianic remnant from the invading armies of the Antichrist. He will destroy them with the sword from His mouth as there will be blood as high as a horse's bridle for a hundred and eighty miles in the Valley of Decision. As Zechariah prophecies of the return, the remaining Jews will look up and wail "as a mother that has lost her child" from seeing the One they had pierced.

Prophecies about the Returning Messiah.

- **His Ascension**
  "Men of Galilee," they said. "Why do you stand here looking into the sky? This same Jesus, who has been taken from you into heaven, will come back in the same way you have seen him go into heaven. (Acts 1)
- **His Return from Heaven**
  He would come again from the clouds of heaven as the Son of Man. (Daniel 7)
- **His Return in Glory**
  He would be the Sun of Righteousness" for all who revere Him and look for His coming again. (Malachi 4)
- **His Return as Israel Repents**
  He is the One whom Israel will finally recognize to be the One they pierced, causing bitter grief. (Zechariah 12)
- **The Conquering Messiah**
  Together they will go to war against the Lamb, but the Lamb will defeat them because he is Lord of all lords and King of all kings.(Revelation 17)

Understanding the Fruit from Suffering

1 Peter 4

Therefore, since Christ suffered in his body, arm yourselves also with the same attitude, because whoever suffers in the body is done with sin. As a result, they do not live the rest of their earthly lives for evil human desires, but rather for the will of God.

"Evidence that our will has been broken is that we begin to thank God for that which once seemed so bitter, knowing that His will is good and that in His time and His way, He is able to make the most bitter waters sweet."
D.L. Moody

After spending over three decades with hurting incarcerated kids, the toughest and most asked question was, "Why does God let bad things happen to good people?" The source of this question is always in the question, "If God exists, "why has he let these things happen to me?" The real answer comes from the cross of the Lamb in the form of sin when Jesus cried out to the Father in agony, "My God, my God, why have you forsaken me?" All of the witnesses marveled from doubt, for the utterance was not meant for "the ears of men."

This is the only place in the Bible where Jesus didn't call Him Father, because Jesus rightly felt forsaken by His Father at that moment. This was the greatest suffering of the crucifixion, because it was the first time in eternity that He was separated from a Father that couldn't look at Him. He truly became our sin. Jesus not only endured the separation from the Father's fellowship, He received the wrath deserved for sinful humanity.

Jesus experienced the greatest suffering to the heart and soul in personal experience in the form of betrayal. A true definition of betrayal is "violation through unfaithfulness." Today, the betrayal of God and of one another has become an art form. It is actually rooted in denying and betraying who we truly are by justifying and lying. As Jesus compelled us "to deny ourselves, to pick up our cross, and follow him," we continue to do the opposite.

This brings us to the point of all of our suffering. It is futile to try to provide answers to such questions without an eternal perspective. As we continue to question God, do we understand this all comes from our personal and corporate defect and wanting another answer than confession and repentance. All of the answers are found within the pages of the Bible, and the intimacy of the Holy Spirit. Suffering is not just consequence for sin, although some seem to think so, it is our greatest weapon for our delivery. Jesus loves us for who we are, but He loves us enough to not leave us there.

How do we find hope through suffering without it only being tied to a specific outcome. Our hope is not that our circumstances will turn out a certain way, or that God will give me exactly what you want, but it is knowing God will always do what is best for us. It is our living hope in a Savior who loves me, not in release. Being happy comes from the root, "happen." We must shift to "the joy of the Lord being our strength" because it is rooted and grounded in eternity. We need to learn live out trusting our Savior and our Lord as ambassadors of truth.

Every day the mirror seems to speak from Paul, "though our outward man is perishing, our inward man is being renewed day by day." We all bear momentary affliction that at times seems unbearable. Paul tells us to not lose heart, but look toward the unseen and eternal will of God. Paul's example revealed that suffering was for the tempering of our soul and our character; an opportunity to strengthen and transform our inner being. This is why the Book of Job is so misunderstood. It is a deep mystery often beyond our comprehension. I wonder whether or not many people under today's pressure grasp for the answer, or do they just walk until the road ends. You cannot accept the conquering King until you receive the redeeming Lamb of God.

Israel violated their covenant in the desert through unbelief as they refused to understand they were shattering God's heart. They never learned their suffering travel was to refine them for the preparation for the Promised Land. They not only rejected and betrayed their Lord; they had betrayed themselves. In the Book of Romans, Paul declared, "If God is for us, who can be against us?" A harder question for Israel and the prodigal church is, "If God is against us, who can be for us?" Have we learned this warning, or are we repeating it?

Understanding the Fruit of Obedience

Hebrews 5

During the days of Jesus' life on earth, he offered up prayers and petitions with fervent cries and tears to the one who could save him from death, and he was heard because of his reverent submission.

"Then it gets us out of the sanctuary into the world into places of obeying and loving ordering our lives as living sacrifices in the world to the glory of God. There is a lot involved, all the parts of our lives out on the street participating in the work of salvation." Eugene Peterson

Obedience is our connection to trusting and respecting our Lord. It actually comes from a Latin word meaning "to hear." When we obey God, it is a sign that we really trust Him and are listening to what He is saying, and responding. We do not have to guess what is right and what is wrong, because God always tells us exactly what we need to do, to keep us from falling back into sin. Obedience to God is not only a way to worship Him, but a way of intimacy. As Christians, we know we are not saved by our works because "our faith without works is dead". Obeying God should not be a burden but pure joy, a way of worshipping him and growing in the faith.

Obedience is the opposite of the lawlessness that is mastering the planet. The Apostle Paul was already weeping over many that became "enemies of the cross of Christ." Their destiny would be destroyed by their senses and their glory would become their shame in reaping what they had sown. This explosion in rejecting the cross, is forsaking any boundary or commitment to Christ, putting "selfism" on the throne.

This spirit of disobedience is even manifesting in the prodigal church through carnal desire. Paul directly warned us in the Book of Titus, "To the pure, all things are pure, but to those who are corrupted and do not believe, nothing is pure. In fact, both their minds and consciences are corrupted. They claim to know God, but by their actions they deny him. They are detestable, disobedient and unfit for doing anything good." It is paramount that we understand there is no neutral ground.

Our first response to the current events as a believer today is to be filled with terror. The ancient quote. "the road to hell is paved with good intentions" is graphic definition of the Messiah's warning of the broad road leading to destruction. It has no boundaries; no moral conviction and it appears to have no price because the toll booth is at the end of the road. It is broadening every moment. The truth is if we pick up our cross and follow Christ in obedience, redemption will follow. You must realize that the true church will be rescued to Christ when He finally removes the only thing "restraining" the spirit of disobedience.

CHAPTER THREE
The Concurring Rejection of the Messiah

The true light that gives light to everyone was coming into the world. [10] He was in the world, and though the world was made through him, the world did not recognize him. He came to that which was his own, but his own did not receive him. Yet to all who did receive him, to those who believed in his name, he gave the right to become children of God, children born not of natural det, nor of human decision or a husband's will, but born of God. The Word became flesh and made his dwelling among us. We have seen his glory, the glory of the one and only Son, who came from the father, full of grace and truth.

"The only sin God cannot forgive is the sin of rejecting Christ. Turn to Him in repentance and faith and He will forgive you." Billy Graham

As the Messiah bled from the cross, the sifting process of betrayal was activated. His rejection sealed the fate that led to the fall of the Roman empire from within, and it led Israel to the desert of the Diaspora. This very cross continues to sift the globe with this very choice that all will have to make. In the Book of Philippians, Paul's voice echoed through the streets of Rome declaring the divinity of Jesus when he declared that "every knee will bow and every tongue will confess Jesus Christ as Lord. This final verdict is finally written in the blood of the indicted in the Valley of Decision.

The insurrection of betrayal and rejection began with King Herod invoking his soldiers to slaughter thousands of innocent male children in Bethlehem in an attempt to kill the Christ child whom Herod feared would eventually seize his kingdom. From here, the blind and twisted hatred from the prince of Darkness knew no bounds, yet his foolish schemes only opened the door for salvation.

The Gospel of John stretches further back than the Book of Genesis. The Apostle John spoke first of the eternal Messiah coming to His own, but they would reject Him. Hecame to save humanity, but appeared first to His chosen people of Israel. He came and lived among them, and initially it was them he was sent to. The Jews by this time had become a hardened, judgmental people never healing from the wounds of their past. Again, their nation had fallen under the brutal fist of Rome, but Jesus Christ was compassionately truthful to them about their sifting condition was written in their history.

To summarize the veil of unbelief, Israel had the very oracles of God which foretold them beforehand when and where to expect the Messiah and of what tribe he would arise. He came among them, introduced signs and wonders, and revealed Himself as the Messiah; yet they never received Him. They rejected his teaching, they did not welcome him as their Messiah, but fortified themselves against him through religious pride and conceit. Behind their walls, they were slowly perishing in unbelief into the coming terror of the Diaspora.

After Israel had spent several centuries desperately waiting and anticipating their Messiah's arrival on their terms, the masses of Israel didn't even recognize Him face to face. There was a veil over the face of their nation and their souls. After eons of exile and occupation, they only desired a political king that would rescue them from their enemies. Israel rejected Christ's teaching that He was the only door to redemption, in fact, they believed they had no need for a mediator to reach back to God. They ignored and regarded forgiveness as inferior to their temporal restoration.

Israel rejected Jesus Christ as their Messiah from their sin of unbelief. The core of ignorance was their unbelief that the Messiah would be the Lord Himself. They found it inconceivable that the Lord God funneled Himself into a virgin and walked among them, even though the prophets had spoken it. Their pride in the Law and their heritage had blinded them as with Lucifer, that they considered "they were the reason for their own brightness." By the Lord's providence, they were blinded concerning the Messiah's presence so the gate of salvation would then be open to the Gentiles. This began another cycle of humanity refusing the love and truth from God to further their own devices. They would reap the harvest from the seed of arrogance they had sown with the coming Diaspora scattering them to the wind, and being exiled again under the boot of the gentiles whom they hated. Though they fell hard, the Messiah would eventually bring them home from their testing.

There are many of the same questions to ask concerning the hour of trial we are entering. As we stand before the gates of the Tribulation, who will be taken home? What can we receive from God's Word and His Spirit to not betray our Messiah and King? What part can we have in the repentance and revival of Israel and the lukewarm nominal church? When will God's grace and patience eventually run dry again as it did at the entry of the Great Deluge? I do know this. The rejection of the Messiah as Savior leaves you with no help and no hope. We must find our knees first if we are ever to stand again. As we are perishing, we have lost the keys to His Kingdom?

Kicking Against the Prick.

Acts 9

Meanwhile, Saul was still breathing out murderous threats against the Lord's disciples. He went to the high priest and asked him for letters to the synagogues in Damascus, so that if he found any there who belonged to the Way, whether men or women, he might take them as prisoners to Jerusalem. As he neared Damascus on his journey, suddenly a light from heaven flashed around him. He fell to the ground and heard a voice say to him, "Saul, Saul, why do you persecute me?" "Who are you, Lord?" Saul asked. "I am Jesus, whom you are persecuting," he replied. "Now get up and go into the city, and you will be told what you must do

The keys to the Kingdom were discovered by the most cruel culprit that was unleashing the brutal persecution of the pioneering church. The scripture has given us two priceless revelatory examples concerning the crisis of unbelief that began with Israel. The second was Saul, the pharisee that had sold his soul for religion and power. The history of the Apostle Paul was laced with the prideful way of the Pharisees, and the brutal way of the Romans. His heart was divided by the distorted theocracy that had poisoned Israel, and the sorcerous power of Rome. It took the Lord of Glory to break him and remake him as a first fruit of Messianic hope. As he wrote in the Book of Romans, "And we know that in all things God works for the good of those who love him, who have been called according to his purpose." He is the most profound witness in the Bible for us to understand the ultimate power of the cross.

Paul was Jewish, born in the Roman city of Tarsus. He had a harshness and rigidity from the Roman culture. He was extremely proud of his Jewish heritage, so he chose to use his Hebrew name Saul, until his radical conversion. This provoked his skepticism and hatred for the son of a carpenter. Paul considered Jesus to be a false prophet radicalizing a false religion that was in direct conflict with the Jewish tradition he so devoutly followed. He was so zealous for Judaism, and so against this new perceived cult. His mission was a crusade to brutally persecute Christians from the Way.

The Book of Acts contains three accounts of Paul's conversion giving different facets of his incredible salvation. We are given beautiful detail with differing perspectives for this man of passion that had to be broken like all of us, for him to be the vessel to pioneer his apostleship in the Messiah. These accounts demonstrate the reliability of being identical yet having varied facets. Depending upon the purpose for telling a story and the audience that will hear it, people choose to emphasize different aspects of the story.

The First Account (Acts 9)

After being the ringleader in persecuting Christians in Jerusalem and Judea, Saul obtained permission from the high priest, to set out for Damascus, hoping to scourge and arrest Christians who had fled persecution. On his way, Paul and his companions suddenly witnessed a great, blinding light from above. Paul fell to the ground and heard Jesus' voice, asking why Saul was persecuting Him. After the blinding revelation, the Lord commanded the believer named Ananias to meet Saul and to minister to him. Despite his great fear from knowing Saul's reputation Ananias obeyed. Saul, soon to be known as Paul, regained his sight and began his ministry.

Something like scales fell from his eyes, he regained his sight, and he was baptized. Paul first had to be viciously grounded and then the Light came from heaven and blinded him. He knew this had to be from God, and then he heard from his least expected Source. This was the beginning process from his Master to save Saul from himself.

The Second Account (Acts 22)

The second account was Paul's testimony during his trial before the Jews. After years of preaching Christ throughout Asia Minor and Greece, Paul had returned to Jerusalem. He was falsely accused of bringing a Gentile into the temple and he was arrested. As Paul addressed his accusers, he reflected back on his conversion, and told them that he was a Jew, brought up and educated under the famous Jewish teacher Gamaliel. He recounted his zeal in persecuting Christians and his mission to Damascus. Paul finally described the bright light and the voice of Christ, and quoted Jesus as saying, "I am Jesus the Nazarene whom you are persecuting."

A true witness was born with an undeniable conviction. He humbly repented and with passion began to impact other in the way he never had. He began to exchange his legalistic fervor, for the grace from his previous Adversary. He also experienced the persecution he so willfully inflicted upon others. Paul quickly became a flaming evangelist more clearly and powerfully than any other.

The Third Account (Acts 26)

This account is significantly different from the other two. In this case, Paul had been in prison for over one year and he had been testifying in his own defense before the Judean King Agrippa. Paul described his persecuting Christians in much greater detail. He added details about the encounter on the road, including that "it is hard for you to kick against the pricks." Jesus told Paul that he was chosen by God and that he would bring the gospel to the Gentiles, all in great detail.

This account is primarily focused on Christ's confession of denying God's authority. "It is hard for you to kick against the pricks" was a Greek proverb that was also familiar to the Jews and anyone who understood agriculture. It was a long stick with a pointed piece of iron on its tip used to prod the ox is being disobedient. The farmer would prick the animal to steer it forward in the right direction. If the animal would rebel by kicking out at the goad, the prick would be driven even further into its flesh. There is a powerful lesson in the ancient Greek proverb. Solomon wrote, "Stern discipline awaits him who leaves the path" when we choose to disobey God, we become like the rebellious ox, driving the goad deeper and deeper.

Paul's Continuing Passion for His Fallen Nation

Romans 10

Brothers and sisters, my heart's desire and prayer to God for the Israelites is that they may be saved. For I can testify about them that they are zealous for God, but their zeal is not based on knowledge. Since they did not know the righteousness of God and sought to establish their own, they did not submit to God's righteousness. Christ is the culmination of the law so that there may be righteousness for everyone who believes.

The Apostle Paul was branded through his conversion, yet he never forgot his engraving from Israel. He understood their horrific position because he was the worst offender before God's mercy. It positioned Paul to be a reluctant defender for Israel because the Lord had enlightened him over Israel's fall.

The greatest witness from the Apostle Paul came when he went from holding the hammer to holding the nails as he experienced the persecution from his own that eventually cost him his head. Yet, with Paul's unswerving loyalty to his native heritage, he never abandoned his heart for his people or his nation. He stood there with the remnant chosen through grace as he understood the Lord was not finished with Israel. God had given Israel "a spirit of stupor, blindness, and deafness" that still lingers. In light of God's multitude of promises to Israel, could God's promises have failed? This spirit is slowly being removed with the Messiah.

As the Apostle Paul wept deeply over the rejection of Jesus Christ by Israel, he exclaimed that he would exchange his own redemption for the salvation of his countrymen, because he understood they did not stumble as to fall beyond recovery. Paul spoke, "Not at all! Rather, because of their transgression, salvation has come to the Gentiles to make Israel envious." The prodigal church should look intensely into this lesson and not reject Israel because God never has.

Sadly, from this age, the historic error in Christianity divorces Israel from their covenant which would invalidate uncountable prophecies in eschatology. Replacement theology is the view that the church is the new and true Israel that has permanently replaced or superseded Israel as the people of God. This heresy has been the fuel that has helped energize grave error and separation for centuries and now blurs the meaning of the modern state of Israel, and the current events in the Middle East.

It continues to inflame the anti-Semitism in Europe and entice the hideous denial that the Holocaust was a myth. Wherever replacement theology had flourished, the Jewish people have had to run for cover. This is now raging over the entire planet. Replacement theology has declared the Church as the seed of Abraham. This is not only heretical; it projects God to be unfaithful. The truth is God will never forsake His peoples or His promises and neither should we. It is evident Israel is percolating in prophecy, and will soon triumph after the completion of the church age.

The confessors of replacement theology have no specific future plan for the nation of Israel, except for "driving them into the sea of forgetfulness." This heresy teaches that the church is the replacement for Israel and that the many promises made to Israel in the Bible are fulfilled in the Christian church, not in Israel. The prophecies in Scripture concerning the blessing and restoration of Israel to the Promised Land are spiritualized or allegorized into promises of God's blessing for the church.

Contrary to replacement theology, after the rapture the church age will end as God will return to Israel as the primary focus of His plan. In one way or another, our nation and the churches' days are numbered. In the Book of Revelation, Christ warns the church to "Remember, therefore, what you have received and heard; hold it fast, and repent. But if you do not wake up, I will come like a thief, and you will not know at what time I will come to you." I must add the torment for this moment, as the boiling pot is tipping. for the first time in our nation's history, we are falling under God's curse for betraying Israel for twisted motives. If there is no repentance, there will be no forgiveness.

Is the Church Rejecting Their Messiah?

You have persevered and have endured hardships for my name, and have not grown weary. [4] *Yet I hold this against you: You have forsaken the love you had at first. Consider how far you have fallen! Repent and do the things you did at first. If you do not repent, I will come to you and remove your lampstand from its place.*

"It is doubtful whether God can bless a man greatly until He has hurt him deeply." A.W. Tozer

We are at one of the most critical conjunctures at this moment in understanding what is also happening in the sifting of the church. The constant process of sifting a remnant has been happening since the garden of Eden. It continued with the sifting process of Israel as they refused their mission to the nations. Today, it has finally returned with the remnant being sifted from the "nominal" church. Please understand the definition of "nominal." In Webster's Dictionary it is stated to be the "existing or being something in name or form only." The fragmentation and the church abandoning its mission like Israel has left us in the same position. Understand, this will surface throughout the rest of the book with greater importance.

Once again, a tragic example was set in the first church of Ephesus in the Book of Revelation. It was birthed in the era of the catacombs and caves hiding from vicious persecution from the Romans and Judaism as Christ walked in their midst. They suffered in beauty and refused the apostasy that was already at work. Tragically, they forgot their calling and their reason. After being warned, this church was removed because they left their first love. This has returned again and again through the church age and we are suffering from its last stage and it cannot be denied.

The inverted digression of these prophetic churches in the Book of Revelation gives us a deeper revelation by specific example with the church in Laodicea. Ironically, Laodicea means "the people's rights" and aptly describes the seventh and last period of the history of a professing nominal church, It is a time when the masses are rising up and claiming their rights and blessings before their God.

This church was lukewarm, and indifferent with a self-sufficient attitude. They claimed to be rich and have need of nothing, but they were wretched, pitiful, poor, blind and naked. They were challenged by Christ to buy gold tried in the fire of conviction." Gold tried in the fire" is a symbol of divine sifting. This arises from despising the testimony to the Lord's Name and rejecting the light of truth. It was a testament to the isolation from the Lord and their willingness to follow the ways of the world.

The Lord stands outside knocking and has taken a place outside of the Church of Laodicea, a solemn thing indeed. Its wretched moral state compelled Him to assume this position. He is also warning them of the rebuke and discipline that was to come. In fact, there is nothing positive that our Lord has to say about Laodicea. The irony is the fact that they thought they were perfect, but they were truly blind to their own condition. The greatest sin here was that they had stopped listening and that they were in love with the sound of their own voice. They had not only shut the door to His presence but they were playing the harlot in the world.

As the Apostle Paul had to stand against his heritage and ritualistic religion, we are now challenged with the identical fall of our nation into a revived rebellion in a post-Christian America. As he despaired over the rampant idolatry, it was the Gospel of love that provoked him to act in truth. Shackled in hope of his eternal values. he saw the damning impact in their lost culture as the futility of dead religion embraced his spiritual heritage. The nominal church is now repeating the history of the Jewish bondage, but in reverse.

As Israel, the nominal church does not want the Messiah to be their king, they want him to be their sugar daddy. The plea, "Lord, take my problem, but not my sin" is raging through spiritual apathy. This mentality has shackled the witness of the nominal church into compromise and shame. The mantra, "If you stand for nothing, you will fall for anything" is as serious about devotion as it is for vision. As in Israel's demise, today's apostasy is the act of defecting from continuing to follow, obey, or acknowledge the Messiah as Savior and more importantly as our King. To fully identify and combat apostasy, we must understand the rampant, various forms of heresy and to characterize and warn against its doctrines and teachings.

The Cankerworm at the Root

Now, LORD, take away my life, for it is better for me to die than to live." But the LORD replied, "Is it right for you to be angry?" had gone out and sat down at a place east of the city. There he made himself a shelter, sat in its shade and waited to see what would happen to the city. Then the LORD God provided a leafy plant and made it grow up over Jonah to give shade for his head to ease his discomfort, and Jonah was very happy about the plant. But at dawn the next day God provided a worm, which chewed the plant so that it withered. When the sun rose, God provided a scorching east wind, and the sun blazed on Jonah's head so that he grew faint. He wanted to die, and said, "It would be better for me to die than to live.

Matthew 12

He answered, "A wicked and adulterous generation asks for a sign! But none will be given it except the sign of the prophet Jonah. [40] For as Jonah was three days and three nights in the belly of a huge fish, so the Son of Man will be three days and three nights in the heart of the earth. [41] The men of Nineveh will stand up at the judgment with this generation and condemn it; for they repented at the preaching of Jonah, and now something greater than Jonah is here.

I painted the above image of the reluctant prophet Jonah and it is called "Jonah's Wail" to reflect our fall as a nation and a church. It reveals him embracing an idol as the wicked and adulterous Ninevah in their settled rebellion. Jonah was about to be swallowed up, not just by a whale, but his own unrepentant heart.

Jonah wanted Ninevah to die in their sin without realizing that he was dying in his own. The story of Jonah was not just a warning to Ninevah, it led to Israel standing before Jesus seeking a sign instead of their redeeming Messiah, leading them to share in the same judgement as their enemy.

"Jonah's wail" began as the word of the Lord came to Jonah. God commanded "Jonah to go to Nineveh; and cry out against its sin and rebellion and call them to repentance." Jonah refused and rebelled because he hated Ninevah and he went the opposite direction. The sifting process began in the belly of a pagan ship as the Lord sent a raging storm. Jonah's response was to hide in sleep as the storm fermented. Perhaps the storm outside even seemed insignificant in comparison to the storm inside of Jonah . The nature of his sleeping is all to revealing, and too much like the sleep of the nominal Christian today. Jonah slept in a place where he hoped no one would see or disturb him while he was drunk on self-pity.

Jonah woke up in a moment of clarity as he realized this storm was going to kill everyone on board because of his sin, so he asked to be tossed into the sea. He finally realized he was the real problem. The apex of terror came as he was swallowed by a whale. This was his rescue, not his demise. As Jonah was to call Ninevah to repentance, Jonah was then swallowed alive by a whale representing his heart of stone, refusing to repent and do God's will. He was then vomited out of the mouth of the whale.

I have prepared a supplementary art piece of Jonah being saved through fire. As Jonah leaves the city of Ninevah, he is sulking in in fury as he is sitting under the shade tree the Lord provided as another lesson. The leaves had withered from a devouring cankerworm at the roots of the shade tree as he sits under the scorching sun, allowing Jonah a plant that became a "shadowing idol." How often our idols are allowed to perish to teach us the deeper lesson. The Lord will take us to the end of all things to propel us to repent.

It has now become a parable for our nation and today's nominal church. Jonah exemplified the same disobedience to the Gospel and wanted to sulk in his own comfort as the lost perished. As we began, the final lesson of Jonah is revived in the critical warning from Christ concerning the metaphor of Jonah. The "sign of

Jonah" given by Jesus was not just a call for those in front of Him to repent, but it rings even louder today. Jesus warned there would be just one sign given of His Messiahship; "the sign of Jonah." This was given to any evil generation that seeks a sign instead of God. Jesus simply called to repentance. Jesus denied their seeking after a sign, especially when countless signs had already happened before their eyes. Jonah was the sign of a prophet in a sense far beyond his preaching to Nineveh; he prophesied the death and resurrection of Jesus. This sign revealed His coming death, His coming resurrection, and the coming sifting.

Many nations have been destroyed or conquered suddenly in history, time and again. Many nations have slowly crumbled from within before their demise. Are we a nation on the instant path of destruction as the empire of Babylon? Are we a nation on the same crumbling path as the empire of Roman empire? Having God's favor upon a nation always depended on their faith producing the fruit of moral character. God's moral law applies not only to a nation, but especially to the individual. Will humanity or will we ever learn the lessons from history and return to the Lord and Savior? We are in a severe battle on two fronts. The desecration of our nation and the nominal church are abandoning the heritage we once valued. It is boiling down to personal devotion.

The Roman philosopher, Cicero said, "A nation can survive its fools, and even the ambitious, but it cannot survive treason from within. An enemy at the gates is less formidable, for he is known and he carries his banners openly. But the traitor moves among those within the gate freely, his sly whispers rustling through all the alleys, heard in the very halls of government."

An equal treason now lies within the walls of the church. As the treason of Jonah was that Jonah couldn't past himself to get to God, the nominal Christian is repeating Jonah's history. It is the whisper that the idea that after we have become a Christian the moral law of God no longer has any authority over me. This leaven has disarmed the nominal church and the personal witness of too many. The truth is the graver error of lawlessness that is at work on the globe has even intoxicated the church. We can no longer put off "the day of evil" or the returning Messiah "as He comes like a thief in the night." The sifting will come with the matured harvest.

THE SIFTING OF
PLANET EARTH

CHAPTER FOUR
God's Sifting Process from the Beginning

Romans 8

We know that the whole creation has been groaning as in the pains of childbirth right up to the present time. Not only so, but we ourselves, who have the first fruits of the Spirit, groan inwardly as we wait eagerly for our adoption to sonship, the redemption of our bodies. For in this hope, we were saved. But hope that is seen is no hope at all. Who hopes for what they already have? But if we hope for what we do not yet have, we wait for it patiently.

coming out of prison and off the streets, there was a prodigal that had fallen out of his third story apartment window, angry and intoxicated. After weeks in the hospital, he arrived at the facility more wounded on the inside than the outside. He had recently been released from a California prison where Ted Bundy and others resided. His prison face and his brutal gang history had become his only identity. He would come in strutting his prison life day in and day out playing "king on the mountain."

I finally had to confront him, saying "You know what Bill, I am so glad that you survived and made it out of prison, but we now have to find the way to get the prison out of you." He had not lost his identity because he never really had one. He was encamped in the agony of repeating the history of his father. Gangs are based on two false foundations; territory and respect. Like terrorists, they occupy what is not theirs and they try to gain respect through fear.

This tragic deception is a summary of life void of God and the pursuit of the image of God, but how can we be conformed into the image of Christ? As we dwell in the age where the image of the beast is being brought to life, it is the prison that a believer must escape and to get out of him.

We will now begin to get to the heart of the matter. Sifting is the last stage of a harvest season. In the spiritual realm, it is a period of deep pain with the divine purpose of purifying and increasing our faith. Sifting is the process of death and renewal from a life that no longer conforms to the present evil age. This power of transformation can come from only one source. Paul said, "For the message of the cross is foolishness to those who are perishing, but to us who are being saved it is the power of God." Every believer must endure this either today or tomorrow. It determines whether our life is fruitful or barren.

We will now begin with the disciples being prepared for the day of Pentecost where they had come to the end of themselves. When you look on the surface at the disciples it can be perplexing why Jesus chose each one of them, but when I look in the mirror, I have the same response. Amazing grace. When I do an art piece, I always defer to a dark background to make the central image appear bright and distinct. I am amazed at the handiwork that the Lord did with the disciples before their rebirth at Pentecost.

The last Passover that Jesus spent with His disciples has more tragedy than anything. This Last Supper was painted by Leonardo DaVinci to depicts the shock and horror of the twelve disciples upon learning that one amongst them was going to betray Jesus Christ. What they didn't realize was there were two. This was at the point of no return for Judas, and the greatest failure of Peter and the fall of the rest. This began the sifting that continues today. The disciples were blind to their own weakness having not received the Holy Spirit yet. As Jesus warned them of the drastic turn that was coming, the prince of this world was preparing his final assault through Judas Iscariot. They were facing a battle with a far deeper level of conflict as Satan entered the soul of Judas. This would be the hour of darkness they were warned would come.

When Jesus finally exposed Judas for the traitor he was. Judas responded, "surely you don't mean me, Rabbi?" Unlike Peter, his loss was to be an eternal sifting, that he would never recover from. Jesus then told them all, "this very night you will all fall away." Then Peter blindly declared again, "Even if I have to die with you, I will never disown you. Peter insisted that he was far more faithful and he would die for Jesus as others would not. This began a measure of sifting to prepare Peter to be able to fulfil the promise that eventually took his life.

The Deeper Sifting of the Disciples

Luke 22

"Simon, Simon, Satan has asked to sift all of you as wheat. But I have prayed for you, Simon, that your faith may not fail. And when you have turned back, strengthen your brothers." But he replied, "Lord, I am ready to go with you to prison and to death." Jesus answered, "I tell you, Peter, before the rooster crows today, you will deny three times that you know me."

Peter's heart must have been deeply lanced when Jesus warned that Satan wanted to sift him like wheat. How could Peter not understand that his Messiah saw right through his prideful denial. Jesus responded immediately that before the rooster would crow in the morning, Peter would betray Him three times. This was confirmed later in scripture and it was his path of sifting into brokenness. Peter's faith would falter but not fail. Jesus did not see the temporary lapse that was to come as a failure of faith, because He knew that Peter would return to Him through the sifting of his soul. This began the threshing that night that would eventually separate the disciples within and without.

Jesus finally took Peter, James and John to the Garden of Gethsemane to pray in earnest before His arrest. As He anguished to the point of sweating blood, the others fell asleep. He sadly asked them; can you not even stay awake for an hour? Suddenly, Judas came with an army of soldiers from the Pharisees. Going to Jesus at once, Judas greeted Jesus with a kiss. Judas was finally sifted out by his own wicked heart of unbelief. As he identified Jesus with a kiss, addressing him as master, he finally exposed who his master truly was. The sin of Judas was so unnatural and hideous, that it is difficult to understand.

As the Messiah was arrested, Peter drew his sword and struck the ear off of a soldier. Jesus rebuked Peter, and asked

"Could I not have called down a legion of angels?" I am sure Peter then remembered a few days earlier when Jesus said, "I have not come to bring piece but a sword." Jesus knew that Peter's distorted courage would fail him at send him into a tail spin. The context of Christ "not bringing peace but a sword" was not about cutting off ears, but the dire breaking of Peter's soul and strong will.

A final sifting occurred at the Sea of Galilee where Peter had once found his former identity. After Peter's horrific betrayal, Jesus came to restore Peter after His resurrection. As Jesus asked Peter the third time if he loved Him, He said, "Peter, do you truly love Me?" The old Peter would have said, "Oh Lord, I love You. I will die for You!" But the new, transforming Peter humbly replied, "Lord, you know all things, that I love you." A new dawning had arrived where Peter began to exchange his independence for dependence on his Lord, and would eventually hang on his cross upside down.

The Sifting from the Beginning

Genesis 8

Then Noah built an altar to the LORD and, taking some of all the clean animals and clean birds, he sacrificed burnt offerings on it. The LORD smelled the pleasing aroma and said in his heart: "Never again will I curse the ground because of humans, even though every inclination of the human heart is evil from childhood. And never again will I destroy all living creatures, as I have done. "As long as the earth endures, seedtime and harvest, cold and heat, summer and winter, day and night will never cease."

From the very beginning, there was a cankerworm eating at the root of the primal civilization of humanity in the Book of Genesis. Actually, it was a possessed serpent with a hatred for God and His eternal purpose. With his band of fallen angels, they infested the planet with despicable wickedness in the heart of God's new creature. Satan and the fallen angels had seduced and stolen the purpose of Adam into a black hole of self-will with evil on their hearts continually.

This led to the core of the hideous conspiracy with the Way of Cain. This was Satan's arrogant entitlement birthed again in heart of mankind, transfusing the forgetfulness of God as they refused to repent even as they faced the wrath of God. As the seed of rebellion was sown through Cain, it brought great shame and guilt for their original sin, the harvest of this rebellion is manifested in the final order that is culminating today.

The society around the family of Noah was saturated with violence, corruption, and degradation. The spiritual and physical interaction between demonic forces and humans, even the sexual had become perverted with the twisted angels. The fingerprints of the previous offenders were found on the entire generation of Noah, yet Noah found grace in the eyes of His Lord. His family was the first remnant that was sifted from the madness from the first order of rebellion.

In the beginning God created, but in the end, He is sifting. As the waters receded, this critical promise to humanity of not flooding the earth again came from the aroma of Noah's imperfect sacrifice. With only seven of each animal on the ark, Noah risked extinction by sacrificing some of these animals. But costly sacrifice is pleasing to God. This framed the Lord's saying that He would endure the evil heart of man as long as the earth endures seedtime and the harvest. This prophecy goes deep into the issue of sifting for eternal purpose. God desires costly sacrifice from us because it is conforming us into His image, which is not only His original intention but the greatest display of completed sacrifice as His first begotten Son.

The Sifting and Separation of Abraham

Genesis 12

The LORD had said to Abram, "Go from your country, your people and your father's household to the land I will show you.

"I will make you into a great nation,

and I will bless you;

I will make your name great,

and you will be a blessing.

After the baptism of the deluge, the Lord began again with an unexpecting soul from the house of an idolater. Again, God chose someone that no one else would have. As the Lord "looks upon the thoughts and intents of the heart, He saw a heart of obedience in Abraham. Aside from Moses, there is no Old

Testament character mentioned more in the New Testament than Abraham. We can learn a great deal from the special call of God from this patriarch. Abram was called "Abraham the Hebrew" in Genesis, which is the first time that the word is used in the Bible. What is a Hebrew? The word "Hebrew" in the Hebrew language is (Ivrie) which mean "to cross over, or pass through." In the Bible, it primarily refers to being a "river crosser." This is synonymous with passing from darkness to Light by all of the patriarchs.

By all human standards, it was a very strange that Abraham suddenly heard from God to cross over and separate from everything he knew. He left his nation, his home, and his family to go off to a destination appointed by God. This was peculiar in the eyes of the world, but it was very pleasing in the eyes of God. As Abraham was called out of the rebellion near the Tower of Babel, as God's single witness to the continuing fallen world. He was willing to go wherever God led him, while the masses attempted to huddle together in their accustomed space for selfish gain.

The greatest sifting of his faith came about with his son Isaac, the apple of his eye; the one he had waited a century for. He was commanded by God to obey the unthinkable by taking him and placing him on an altar to sacrifice. This would foreshadow what God would do eventually on a cross at Calvary. The agony from Abraham's heart by faith mirrored our Father at His ultimate separation from His own Son.

In every step he took, he must have pleaded for a change of God's heart with some other answer. As Abraham built the altar and arranged the wood, the reality must have been sinking in. Finally, he restrained Isaac, placed him on the altar to plunge the fatal knife into his heart. As he raised the knife to his son Isaac, the Angel of the Lord cried out to Abraham to relent. As he looked up, there in a thicket was the ram of mercy caught by his horns.

Abraham is called "the Father of Faith" for this reason. He underwent the greatest trial of all in human history. It must have been bewildering in pondering sacrificing his only son at his old age. As the Apostle shared, "Abraham believed God, and it was credited to him as righteousness." .

The Sifting and Separation of Moses

Hebrews 11

By faith Moses, when he had grown up, refused to be known as the son of Pharaoh's daughter. He chose to be mistreated along with the people of God rather than to enjoy the fleeting pleasures of sin. He regarded disgrace for the sake of Christ as of greater value than the treasures of Egypt, because he was looking ahead to his reward. By faith he left Egypt, not fearing the king's anger; he persevered because he saw him who is invisible. By faith he kept the Passover and the application of blood, so that the destroyer of the firstborn would not touch the firstborn of Israel.

Over a thousand years after Abraham, the Jews found their exodus from Egypt and the hand of the Pharoah as they were living as slaves in Egypt. Their hidden leader would eventually surface as an escaping baby in a basket adrift in a river falling into the hands of the royal Egyptian family, that were murdering Israel's children to stop their growth in Egypt. The history of Moses was amazing, but dreadful.

The introduction of Moses in the Book of Exodus marked a new beginning in the history and the calling of Israel. Moses was the centerpiece of the Old Testament. He was the man chosen to bring redemption to His people as a foreshadow of the coming Messiah. God specifically chose Moses to lead the Israelites from captivity as the deliverer from Egypt for the salvation of the enslaved nation of Israel into the Promised Land. Other than Jesus, Moses might be the most well-known character in the Bible, and definitely to the Old Covenant.

The life of Moses was one of the most beautiful and poetic stories in the Bible. God's gracious hand was slowly moving to free the Jewish people from the hand the pharaoh of Egypt. This catalyzed as He preserved a Hebrew baby from the slaughter in Egypt to become their deliverer. The name Moses (Moshe in Hebrew) is "son drawn out and Deliverer." As noted, Moses was drawn out of the Nile by pharaoh's daughter. This was the Pharaoh's command to all of his people: "Every boy that is born must be thrown into the river, but let every girl live." This command is the backdrop where Moses, a newborn Hebrew baby boy, is "thrown into the Nile" in a basket like an ark, in token obedience to the pharaoh, yet Moses was taken out of the river by none other than the pharaoh's daughter.

The Sifting Anger of Moses

Isaiah 63

One day, after Moses had grown up, he went out to where his own people were and watched them at their hard labor. He saw an Egyptian beating a Hebrew, one of his own people. Looking this way and that and seeing no one, he killed the Egyptian and hid him in the sand. The next day he went out and saw two Hebrews fighting. He asked the one in the wrong, "Why are you hitting your fellow Hebrew?" The man said, "Who made you ruler and judge over us?"

Over the years, there was cauldron of despair brewing in the soul of Moses. Under the robe of this Egyptian prince was an angry, displaced heart with a soul of agony acting out a life that was driven by displacement. All of the years of being under the thumb of the pharaoh had created resentment and hopelessness. He had the hidden heart of a warrior in the imprisoned body of a slave.

It is rare that a person's character is revealed through his ability to say "No!" Moses was a solitary orphan, stripped of his heritage and deprived of his true purpose. In his childhood, being raised by the pharaoh's daughter, he was trained to be an Egyptian prince. Moses was a type of anti-hero, outside of the box of the stereotyped tribal or national leader. He fit the character of Israel, not Egypt, who were biblically portrayed as being outsiders.

When Moses finally had enough of his Egyptian adoption, the character of Moses became a mystery and a contradiction. When it appeared that Moses had taken leave of all common sense, he chose to identify himself with a band of foreign slaves, rather than to retain an inheritance steeped in the advantages of Egypt. Moses was then broken by his own hand, by taking the life of an Egyptian soldier that drove him into his first forty years of exile in the desert. When pharaoh heard of the murder, he sought to kill Moses. When Moses fled from Pharaoh, he settled in the land of Midian. This brutal journey that was foreign to his accustomed comfort, began his sifting through brokenness to become the coming "deliverer" of Israel. The hand of God remained on Moses even though he was not ready to receive his mantle of redeemer.

God Sifts the Soul of Moses

Exodus 4

Then the LORD said, "Put your hand inside your cloak." So, Moses put his hand into his cloak, and when he took it out, the skin was leprous' it had become as white as snow. "Now put it back into your cloak," he said. So, Moses put his hand back into his cloak, and when he took it out, it was restored, like the rest of his flesh.

The miraculous redemption of Moses began when he heard God through a burning bush. The fire began to brand his heart and to begin the mission to rescue his enslaved people. The first issue was that he had to be rescued through fire first to sift and temper him for his future to rescue his people. After his first forty years of tempering in the desert, Moses grew to know God, but God already knew Moses. This was the moment that exposed him on how much he was going to have to learn for his upcoming mission. This was a critical point when Moses began realize who he was truly dealing with. This is where God took off the gloves and Moses was discovering He is not just God, but the sovereign Lord of hosts.

After the Lord spoke that His name was "I am that I am" the Lord reached into the very heart of Moses to expose the primary issue; his desperate heart. This was displayed when the Lord told Moses to put his hand inside his robe. When he took it out, his hand was white with leprosy. Then God told him to return his hand in his robe and his hand was completely restored. This was a profound, prophetic sign of transformation which has always been the heart of the matter.

The Lord graphically showed Moses the content of his character and the body of death that he was trapped in since he was pulled out of the river in Egypt. This was a parable to Moses from what the prophet Jeremiah declared, "the heart is deceitful above all things, and desperately wicked and who can know it?" There is no hope of turning it around and "getting better' without the loving sifting hand of the Lord. Moses had finally come to the end of himself, but his veiled stubbornness that deepened his unbelief, began to dissolve in his relationship with his Lord. The heart of Moses found peace in the sifting and the conviction that we all facing in the Light.

Moses Sifting the Waters

Then his people recalled the days of old,

the days of Moses and his people—

where is he who brought them through the sea,

with the shepherd of his flock?

Where is he who set his Holy Spirit among them,

who sent his glorious arm of power

to be at Moses' right hand,

who divided the waters before them.

The sifting of Moses led to a great harmony between God and Moses, that eventually brought forth the "Great Exodus" where the hand of God merged with the staff of Moses. This set in motion the prophecy of the coming redemption through Jesus Christ as a new and greater Exodus, patterned after the Exodus story. This confirms the lesson of the Old Covenant being a "foreshadow" of the New Covenant. It defined the deliverance from bondage and oppression to the freedom and dignity of sonship that would even come in the last days to Israel.

The challenge for the exodus actually began when Moses and Aaron first met with the Israeli elders. The Israelites chose to accept the divine calling of Moses. Then Moses and Aaron came before Pharaoh and pled, "Let my people go." This followed with the deep plagues in succession to remove the hand of pharaoh. Moses was able to lead the Israelites out of Egypt from the final crippling plague upon Egypt's firstborn. Egypt reaped the whirlwind from the pharaoh's own mouth, and his command was reversed and visited upon their own children. Moses and Israel left with a portion of the wealth of Egypt and were released out of their slavery heading toward the Promised Land.

A week into the Exodus, the hardening heart of pharaoh exploded as he pursued to destroy Israel on the shore of the Red Sea. The pinnacle of God's deliverance came as Moses stretched out his staff and the sea parted. Israel crossed through as the Egyptian army was drowned behind them. The greater concern was not that they left Egypt; but Egypt had not left them. Their perception that the difficulties would now be behind them was anything but true. As Moses, Israel's heart was about to be exposed with the forty years of sifting in the desert, taking them on a journey to realize they needed to be delivered from themselves. Israel was rescued from the brutal hand of Egypt through the baptism of the Red Sea leading to an even greater trial.

Moses Leads Israel into the Sifting Desert

Hebrews 3

So, as the Holy Spirit says:

"Today, if you hear his voice,

do not harden your hearts

as you did in the rebellion,

during the time of testing in the wilderness,

where your ancestors tested and tried me,

though for forty years they saw what I did.

That is why I was angry with that generation;

I said, 'Their hearts are always going astray,

and they have not known my ways.'

""When all is said and done, the life of faith is nothing if not an unending struggle of the spirit with every available weapon against the flesh." Dietrich Bonhoeffer

With the incredible exodus from Egypt came a greater test than captivity. Israel was to learn the harder lesson about themselves that they were childishly disobedient but their taskmasters of Egypt were not the barrier between them and the Lord; it was sin and unbelief. They had to enter their sifting from their time in the wilderness because they could not learn without painful experiences. The Lord had prepared their path with everything necessary so they would learn how sinful their own hearts were, but they refused to repent. From this point, Moses matured in the courage of his convictions as the children of Israel fell to murmuring against God and blaming Moses.

The children of Israel continued to err in their hearts as their souls wandered from no repentance. In fact, they wandered in the desert for forty years on a two-week journey. They doubted that God had their best interest at heart because they had no vision for their identity, or the existence of God's promises. They had seen God perform the parting of the Red Sea and many miracles, yet they doubted He was adequate for the challenge of delivering them into the Promised Land. They shut out the Lord, because they trusted no one, even Moses. So hard was the heart of Israel that the people even wanted to return to their slavery in Egypt.

When you don't believe God, you don't actually stop believing, you simply stop trusting that leads to adultery with idols. Their greatest failures were to persevere in unbelief and testing God when He should have been testing them. After crossing much of the wilderness, and seeing so many reasons to trust in Him, they always fell short. They lost the war of faith through losing their battles. Their rebellion became so grievous that they created a golden calf to repent back to the gods of Egypt.

A profound metaphor of the contradiction of the children of Israel was answered when Jesus was led into the desert to be tempted by the devil. He fasted for forty days symbolizing the forty years of the testing of Israel. From Christ's profound days of temptation in the desert, the devil's temptations found no way to purchase Jesus. He had no self-interest and no ambition for self-exaltation. He came, rather, "to do the will of Him who sent Him." The victory is sure if we stay within the veil of liberty through the Spirit of the Lord. While we struggle with unbelief and self-deception for a time, they are but a skirmish in the war.

The Apostle Paul picks this message up in the bewildering Book of Hebrews with "how shall we escape if we ignore so great a salvation? Has the nominal church learned this lesson or are we just repeating it? Paul then identifies the lingering Hebrews with same adolescence to grow up and put away the bottle of ritual and idolatry. We have digressed into this same "valley of indecision" that Paul warned us "In fact, though by this time you ought to be teachers, you need someone to teach you the elementary truths of God's word all over again. You need milk, not solid food!"

Moses Finally Lays Down the Law

When the people saw that Moses was so long in coming down from the mountain, they gathered around Aaron and said, "Come, make us gods who will go before us. As for this fellow Moses who brought us up out of Egypt, we don't know what has happened to him." Aaron answered them, "Take off the gold earrings that your wives, your sons and your daughters are wearing, and bring them to me." So, all the people took off their earrings and brought them to Aaron. ⁴ He took what they handed him and made it into an idol cast in the shape of a calf, fashioning it with a tool. Then they said, "These are your gods, Israel, who brought you up out of Egypt."

How tragically ironic and specific was the haunting words that Moses brought down from the mountain as they were about to be sifted, reaping the whirlwind. As Israel's history has become ours, we are watching the shackles of the "new global Egypt" put in place as their boots are on our neck. I have to ask where is the example of Moses today? Where is the Restrainer? The Messiah has already come and He is waiting on us to repent and mature for the coming rapture. He is waiting on us as Moses waited on his children.

While Moses was up on the mountain receiving God's laws, the people were getting anxious down in the desert. Moses had spent forty days up on the mountain with God, and by the end of that time, the people were beginning to think Moses had died or left them. Then the people urged Aaron, to make a god for them to follow as they had embraced in Egypt. The idol Aaron crafted was a calf of gold adorned with the spoils of their jewelry from Egypt.

Aaron then called the people together and told them that the golden calf was the idol who delivered them from Egypt. The people offered sacrifices, engaged in pagan rituals, including orgies to worship to their recovered god as they did in their past. When Moses asked Aaron "What have you done?!" his lame excuse was, "It just came out of the fire like this!" How childish was this?! It was bad enough to have a golden calf the people praised for their escape from Egypt, but the second step down was even worse. Aaron honored and sanctified the idol with animal sacrifices on an altar meant only for the Most High. Even Aaron rode on the coat tail of Moses defaulting back to what the Lord had delivered them from. Aaron and the people had ignored God, but He did not ignore them. Moses pleaded with the Lord as He was going to annihilate them. Incredibly, the Lord repented from their complete judgement which he thought to do to these lawless and unrepentant people.

The anger of God transferred to Moses in his rage as he cast the tablets out of his hands and broke them at the foot of the mountain. Moses turned to Aaron and said, "What did this people do to you that you have brought so great a sin upon them?" There are so many lessons to be learned from this devastating backsliding. Apostasy begins with a defiance of the Lord's established authority into a rebellion, and a breach of faith. It always flourishes when leaders defer to the ones whom they serve, whether it God or greed.

The golden calf was really made of wood and covered with a gold wrapped like skin that claimed to be the skin of the gods. When Moses forced the people to drink water laced with the gold, he was really forcing them to consume the skin of the Egyptian god of Apis. By drinking the water, they showed where their allegiance was. It was not with the God Jehovah, but with Pharaoh and his gods.

Moses then set the standard by stating "Whoever is on the Lord's side, come to me!" Moses gave the people of Israel the opportunity to repent and make a stand for the Lord. The Levites, to their honor, sided with the Lord and with Moses. Sadly, they were the only significant group to come out clearly for God's cause at the golden calf incident. This sifting was perilous, but necessary, as it is today. God gave the Law to bring the understanding of the barrier of righteousness and sin, but it could save no one, nor was it ever meant to.

The Law was the schoolmaster to lead Israel to repentance. Leading to the eventual portals of the hands of the coming Messiah. Even then, they did not repent, but inflicted them in the one whom they pierced." Praise Him that His grace endures forever. There is a grave lesson in this for us who claim the faith; "Who is on the Lord's side? Somehow, it is easier to repent when confronted with hell and other horrible things. Jesus said it best, "No man can serve two masters.

CHAPTER FIVE
The Current Sifting of Israel
Revelation 12

A great sign appeared in heaven: a woman clothed with the sun, with the moon under her feet and a crown of twelve stars on her head. She was pregnant and cried out in pain as she was about to give birth. Then another sign appeared in heaven: an enormous red dragon with seven heads and ten horns and seven crowns on its heads. Its tail swept a third of the stars out of the sky and flung them to the earth. The dragon stood in front of the woman who was about to give birth, so that it might devour her child the moment he was born.

Auschwitz Concentration Camp

In the twelfth chapter of Revelation, there is a cosmic woman that flees into the desert pregnant, as she is pursued by Satan, the dragon of old. She bore the Messiah Child who was to rule all nations with a rod of iron. Her Child was then caught up to God to return again to rescue this woman, Israel. Jesus declared that as the time of the end approaches, the people in Israel will be able to hear the final world war rumble with the epicenter at Jerusalem. Jesus then warns Israel "to flee the wilderness into the mountains for there will be great distress, unequaled from the beginning of the world until now, and never to be equaled again." This battle occurs at the mid-point of the Tribulation, termed "the Troubles of Jacob. This is a spiritual battle fought on the battleground of truth and deception, of fear and faith. This will incite the return of the Messiah. that will end with Israel facing genocide in the Valley of Decision.

World War Two was the hallmark of the prophetic statement from Jesus concerning the emerging "wars and rumors of wars" that would intensify from the "Beginning of Sorrows." In our advanced time, global communication and reporting are instant. The influx of social media is many times biased and based on rumor, but the current national media is just as jaded and full of propaganda. The Greek word for "rumors" simply means "to hear by report." To understand what Jesus is specifically saying we must remember that latter Biblical prophecy is centered on the Messiah and Israel.

As a youngster I witnessed the impact of World War Two at ground zero with my father's exhaustion and wounding from this perilous experience. He would not talk with me about his horrendous experience in World War Two until his last few years. The shrapnel wound in his leg testified of his wounded heart that never healed. One of the last things my father had to do in World War Two was to carry the prisoners that couldn't walk out of the concentration camp at Auschwitz.

When my dad and the allied troops entered Auschwitz, they discovered piles of corpses, bones, and human ashes that testified to the demonic murders of the hostages of Israel. They also discovered Jewish survivors suffering from starvation and disease. Over two thirds of European Jewry had been gassed or martyred. The enormous scope and depravity of the Nazi genocide was then exposed to the nations as Israel just wanted to go home. These deeper scars of Israel took them to the end of the road from the Jewish Diaspora. The sifting of Israel did not end there, it just morphed from the most hideous genocide into the concluding birth pains of today.

The Holocaust was the systematic terrorist persecution of six million European Jewish people by a possessed Hitler and the Third Reich. It ended in 1945 when the Allied Powers defeated them to end World War Two. The seed for the Holocaust was issued by the torment of "antisemitism" from the Diaspora. It was the terror of hatred and the tenet of Hitler's Nazi ideology with his desire for a "new world order." Hitler falsely accused the Jewish people of causing Germany's social, economic, political and cultural problems along with their defeat in World War One. This devilish hypnotism was even more hideous than when Caesar Nero blamed the burning of Rome on Christians when he set the city on fire himself. What is terrifying today is the global terrorist fury of antisemitism that has caught fire everywhere today. Though the antisemitic spirit dimmed for a short span bringing Israel home in 1948, it is now a raging flame again in Europe, the Middle East, and even in this nation.

The perpetuating sifting and trials of Israel stem from the basic conflict between eternal purpose and satanic opposition. The very fact that God selected Israel as His special means of divine revelation has made the nation the subject of specific satanic attack. Satanic hatred for Israel has manifested from the beginning of God's dealings from Abraham and has continued through the entire course of human history, culminating in the twisted final assault by the Antichrist and the Fourth Reich in the Valley of Decision.

Here is a Farmside caption claiming the reason.

"Bummer of a birthmark, Hal."

The Miraculous Rebirth of Israel

Matthew 24

"Now learn this lesson from the fig tree: As soon as its twigs get tender and its leaves come out, you know that summer is near. Even so, when you see all these things, you know that it is near, right at the door. Truly I tell you; this generation will certainly not pass away until all these things have happened. Heaven and earth will pass away, but my words will never pass away.

One of the great miracles of Israel's rebirth was that it happened just three years after the Holocaust ended. From the ashes of the concentration camps, the Jewish people suddenly arose and re-established sovereignty in their ancient homeland. Somehow at their time of greatest weakness, they were empowered in a way that had alluded them for centuries by the hand of God. As Israel achieved its independence in 1948, the Jewish people hailed their event as the realization that the Diaspora had ended the two-thousand-year nightmare to restore the Promised Land.

Immediately following their independence, the five Arab nations of Egypt, Jordan, Iraq, Syria, and Lebanon immediately invaded Israel in what became known as the Arab-Israeli War. Continual baptisms of persecutions and war ensued with the Arabs over control of the Middle East. Clashes between Israelis and Palestinians inflamed the region for decades. This provoked the birth pain of "Aliyah" (the Return) as it continues to grow to this very hour. Thousands of young and older Jews returned home from the United States, Britain, Canada, France, and South Africa after the Six Day War.

The key territories around Israel continued to be a cauldron of contention in daily battles. The greatest dispute is that Israel and Palestine both claim Jerusalem as their capital. While Israel doesn't officially recognize Palestine as a state, more than a hundred United Nations members stand fervently against Israel. The U.N. General Assembly passed more resolutions critical of Israel than against all other nations combined, contributing to what observers call an ongoing bigotry toward the Jewish state as a global hypocrite.

While many people associate antisemitism only with the Holocaust, this hatred and the acts fueled by it did not begin in the 1930s, nor did they end in 1945 when the Nazis were defeated. Jews have been stereotyped, exiled, and violently assaulted based on a wide range of false accusations and assumptions, and they have been mocked for having one God for thousands of years.

For centuries, Israel's journey of being caught between the Rock and a hard place is far deeper than on the surface. These verses from the Book of Deuteronomy speak "Among those nations you will find no repose, no resting place for the sole of your foot. There the LORD will give you an anxious mind, eyes weary with longing, and a despairing heart. ⁶You will live in constant suspense, filled with dread both night and day, never sure of your life. In the morning you will say, "If only it were evening!" and in the evening, "If only it were morning!" because of the terror that will fill your hearts and the sights that your eyes will see." This is a graphic description of the Lord's continual discipline of his son, Israel. In .his chilling prediction of the nation's future sufferings, the Lord makes it clear they will be few in number compared to their enemies.

Israel's Ironic Sifting After the Diaspora

Romans 11

Again, I ask: Did they stumble so as to fall beyond recovery? Not at all! Rather, because of their transgression, salvation has come to the Gentiles to make Israel envious. But if their transgression means riches for the world, and their loss means riches for the Gentiles, how much greater riches will their full inclusion bring!

The true purpose for Israel had been veiled through their stumbling and suffering through the centuries of the Diaspora, as they were confused and sifted by the twisting global fury. The Apostle Paul wept over Israel's fall and their betrayal of their Messiah but he was assured that in the last hour they would be engrafted back to full inclusion. After the church was birthed during the same centuries, a darkening bigotry arose in the midst of the church as they embraced the foolish error to think Israel had been forsaken and replaced by the church. This heresy is still tainting the nominal church and sifting the intention of "one new man" with the Jew and the gentile. Now the Messiah is weeping over the nominal church for betraying Israel as they long for answers. Even our nation at this moment for the first time has turned on Israel through twisted political and blind leadership inviting the cursing from the Lord.

The love of God for Israel is written on every page of the scripture. "He disciplines those that He loves." The perfect example of God's sifting of Israel came through the patriarch that God changed his name to "Israel." The mantle of promise from Abraham was passed from Isaac to Jacob. The name Jacob fit him well in the beginning. Jacob means "to circumvent and overreach." He came out of the womb grabbing his twin brother's heel, fighting for his birthright. Later, after stealing his brother's birthright through deception, he fled into the desert as his brother was trying to kill him. God's grace has completing him even now through his inherited nation.

Ironically, the scoundrel Jacob was the first to receive a vision of the house of God. In the desert from angelic inspiration, Jacob took a rock, and poured oil on it. He then proclaimed "surely this is the house of God, "the gateway to heaven." He then described the house of the Lord as an "awesome and terrible place." Heaven's gate to eternity was opened to him through suffering and dwelling in the presence of our awesome Lord.

Jacob crossed his most critical spiritual river when he was sifted and cleansed through brokenness. That evening, Jacob's entire life was radically changed by the most unexpected visitor. All that night, he wrestled with the mysterious Angel of the Lord not understand that it was the Lord Himself. He was finally crippled and would have to walk with a staff for the rest of his life. When Jacob realized his Adversary, he naturally replied "I will not let you go unless you bless me." His real sifting began at that moment when he was humbled as he repented and acknowledged he was the servant, not the lord. God responded by changing Jacob's name to Israel, meaning "let God prevail." He became an amazing parable speaking to the nation of Israel today. The irony of Jacob becoming Israel is that Israel has now become Jacob by trying to cling to their former temples and the days of old.

The Mount of Olives is barely a stone's throw away from the Temple Mount where they long for the temple to be rebuilt. The Temple has a great and terrible history that will rise again even in a more profound dismal future, because they continue to embrace everything but their Messiah. They will have to learn that this coming Temple will be sanctioned by none other than the Antichrist. They will have to relearn the same lesson of wanting a king like the nations and the price they will have to pay.

It is unprecedented that a people that had been scattered throughout the nations for over two millennia, would return to the exact location where they were birthed. It is mystifying that Israel return home came through one of their current villains, the United Nations. The world had a brief moment of empathy from the global village which was provoked by the final hideous acts from Hitler trying to exterminating the Jewish people from the face of the earth. This will be enforced again as the Antichrist rises from the coming Fourth Reich.

Facing the Present Terror and Tremors in Israel

Luke 13

"O Jerusalem, Jerusalem, the one who kills the prophets and stones those who are sent to her! How often I wanted to gather your children together, as a hen gathers her brood under her wings, but you were not willing! See! Your house is left to you desolate; and assuredly, I say to you, you shall not see Me until the time comes when you say, 'Blessed is He who comes in the name of the Lord!'"

"The trials of Israel have always stemmed from the basic conflict between divine purpose and satanic opposition. Satanic hatred of the seed of Abraham was manifested from the beginning and continues through the entire course of human history culminating in the final rebellion in the end." John F. Walvoord

We have finally reached the point where there will be no "peace and security" for Israel until their Messiah returns. The Holy Land and the surrounding areas are the final focal point for the blade of the Messiah on planet earth. The heathen raging are clueless that their wars are not just against Israel, they are against the God of Israel. In their deception and warfare, they are actually bringing the Messianic Kingdom to fruition.

It has been almost fifty years since the last time Israel was officially at war called the Yom Kippur War in 1973 when she was attacked by Egypt, Syria, and others. But what is happening today is a far different kind of war. The current war is borderless between Israel and Calaphatic Iran and their proxies backed by a global cesspool. It will be lanced by the sharpened point of the Messianic blade as it bursts the bubble contrived through lawlessness.

Years ago, the terrorist group ISIS was yearning to become a borderless caliphate. This has now risen with Iran's warped alliance with "death and hell." While the nominal church sleeps, the lines are forming. All of the kingdoms of the world are placed on a fatal chess board of strategy through a tribalistic global unity to destroy the nation of Israel. Even our nation is making fatal choices as a blinded regime that are betraying the "apple of God's eye."

A reprieve occurred in 2020, for a new hope for peaceful resolution led by the United States, Israel and Saudi Arabia. This was a budding treaty called the Abraham Accords that surfaced to promote interfaith and cultural dialogue to advance peace among the supposed three Abrahamic religions in the volatile Middle East. This treaty was signed, but never came to fruition from drowning in politic dispute and dramatic trials that began the threshing from the arriving horses of the apocalypse.

In this same year of the Abraham Accords treaty, the contrived COVID virus was launched in the Wuhan Lab in China, where it was known for developing biochemical weaponry. This was responsible for over sixty million deaths just in 2023. This enacted the "fourth pale horse of the apocalypse" as it rides again to further the path to the Tribulation and to thwart the prospect of peace in the Middle East. This horse carries plagues which is defined as "pestilence and disease" from the fourth seal. Soberly, "pestilence" in the Greek is termed "epidemic leading to pandemic." This satanic assault turned the key to open the global morass and the paradigm shift that now covers the globe with a worldwide web.

The second horse of the apocalypse returned triggering a horrid response to disrupt any hope of an alliance of peace in the Middle East. The core of the problem arose when the tribalistic heart of power and control came again from the continual faction between the Sunnis and Shias. These two tribal nations that compete for the leadership of Islam are Sunni Saudi Arabia and Shia Iran. The radicalized theocracy of Iran panicked over a resurgence of the Abraham Accords in 2023 and turned their fury upon Israel to disrupt the treaty through their possessed proxies. Iran was planning a war with the coalition from their devilish proxies to stop the treaty for peace.

On October 7, 2023, the prophetic clock began to spin wildly as the global chessboard reset as we reached an incredible advance in the war of terror upon Israel. The fragile coalition of Iran's proxies and their plan fractured when the terrorist group, Hamas jumped the gun. The Hamas terrorists rose from the pit and brutally murdered, raped, burned people alive, decapitated babies, and kidnapped hundreds of children, women, men, and the elderly beginning the war to drive Israel into the ocean.

The global spiritual compass completely inverted, never to be the same again until the return of the Messiah. The "Pandora's Box of violent war was opened and will not be shut until the Valley of Decision. Of all things, this hideous and twisted act of terrorism launched a global wave of "antisemitism" in violent hatred not seen since the Holocaust or ever. Even more astounding is that three in four Palestinians believe the wicked attack by Hamas on Israel were justified. How can you justify cutting the heads of babies and raping women to death unless it is satanically inspired. We are truly facing a global pandemic of amoral ideology that we were warned would come. So, who is the victim? Think about it.

This event matched the despicable Herod bringing the genocide of thousands of babies over fear of the coming Messiah. It is the same satanic heartbeat of fear and terror for power's sake. These possessed beasts have no fear of God as they destroy innocent babies in justification. We need to ask how has this overtaken our borders as an invasion? What is stunning is the antichrist spirit that has consumed our universities that is derived from the sorcery in social media. No wonder the name "TikTok" is the sound of a bomb about to explode and a clock running out.

The final birth pains of war are contracting violently on a global level and they will not pause. The quote, "from the river to the sea " has opened the door to the concurrent final two wars. The prophet Ezekiel warned of the "Gog Magog War" that precedes the "Battle of Armageddon" where its pieces of Russia, Iran, and the Arabic nations are already in place. The hooks have already been set in the jaw of Russia (Gog and Magog are identified as Communist Russia and China) as they lead a coalition to the invasion of Israel. This has led Israel to a desperation for peace at any cost as the advent that consummates with "the Troubles of Jacob."

We will detail the final battle in the Valley of Decision later as I leave you with the prophet Zechariah when he spoke for God saying, "I will make Jerusalem like an intoxicating drink that makes the nearby nations stagger when they send their armies to besiege Jerusalem and Judah. On that day I will make Jerusalem an immovable rock. All the nations will gather against it to try to move it, but they will only hurt themselves" As we witness the terrorist global rebellion and the spiritual assault upon Israel, we need to understand, we will be called as a witness at the throne of God. Will you be a witness for the defense or the prosecution?

Facing the Unrepentant Heart of Israel

Jeremiah 4

This is what the LORD says to the people of Judah and to Jerusalem:

"Break up your unplowed ground

and do not sow among thorns.

Circumcise yourselves to the LORD, circumcise your hearts,

you people of Judah and inhabitants of Jerusalem,

or my wrath will flare up and burn like fire

because of the evil you have done,

burn with no one to quench it.

"There must be a deep ploughing, and the eradication of that which hinders growth, both in the realm of the spirit and in nature, before there can be a bountiful harvest." P. Cundall

Israel has entered a time of testing and sifting that has not existed since the days of Jesus the Messiah's first advent. The ground of the Middle East is being shaken and ploughed up to bring forth the fruitful remnant of Israel. As this is also happening with the silent church, the true field that must be sifted is the heart of the individual soul. It simply begins with confessing sin as you turn from it. It is the axis of repentance. It involves recognizing that you have lived wrong in the past and you are determined to live right for the future. True repentance is prompted by "godly sorrow," that "leads to salvation." It has always been and always will be about the cross of Christ declaring the eternal Gospel.

This has been the missing key for Israel as they have habitually rejected the first prophetic suffering vein of the Messiah. The Lord initiated the prophets in the midst of Israel's settled rebellion to plough up the corporate hardened heart. Tradition testifies that Isaiah and many of the other prophets were martyred. Yet they patiently preached repentance to hardened sinners, calling Israel to embrace justice and mercy even as the people stubbornly refused. This is why the prophets were scorned and persecuted to the point of even being sawn in two in a log.

The prophet Jeremiah spoke from the fire in his heart and the fire in his bones over Israel's rejection and betrayal of their Lord. The fire was the purging Holy Spirit within him and pleading for repentance. At one point in his life, Jeremiah was arrested on a charge of desertion and placed into prison. How ironic that Israel would then be charged for the desertion of God by Jeremiah. The prophet Jeremiah then carried the warning to his people to stop their backsliding ways and to return to Him. He warned Israel to "break up your unplowed ground and stop sowing among thorns." This has been the witness of rejection from generation after generation as Israel denies their internal condition, and dwelling in habitual sin. They continue as an unpruned vine bearing no fruit of repentance. Israel will no longer be allowed to be in this state because the slogan that "necessity is the mother of invention" has come to bare.

Israel's Messiah wore a "crown of thorns" pressed into his skull to mock His crown as a king. This brings us back to the beginning. The warning, "do not sow among thorns" refers to the curse upon Adam where the ground would produce no fruit, but "thorns and thistles." We must understand the penalty imposed upon Adam and Eve impacted not just them, but every single person in history as it now rests upon the brow of Israel and the prodigal church.

The thorn is not just a symbol of pain and cursing. A thorn is far more than what sticks you with discomfort. A thorn in reality is an immature, closed-off branch that can bear no fruit. It is one of the most ancient symbols in the world, together with the rose. It is the substance of the pain and pleasure from the tree of knowledge, and far more than something that causes irritation and annoyance. It reflects the unredeemed "selfism" and an imploding immature branch leaving it barren. In contradiction, the thorn is the emblem of Christ's passion as He received humbling crown of thorns to redeem us from ourselves.

The prophet Micah testified, "The best of them is like a brier, the most upright worse than a thorn hedge. The day God visits you has come, the day your watchmen will sound the alarm. Now is the time of your confusion." Spiritually speaking, Israel must repent and return home as a prodigal lost in the lost world. They must stop rending their garments and put their effort into having a circumcised heart. He switches metaphors, leaving the idea of an unplowed field to the idea of circumcised heart, returning to the obedience in the covenant of Abraham.

CHAPTER SIX

The Current Sifting of Our Nation

Jeremiah 2

Has a nation ever changed its gods?

(Yet they are not gods at all.)

But my people have exchanged their glorious God

for worthless idols. Be appalled at this, your heavens,

and shudder with great horror,"

declares the LORD.

"My people have committed two sins:

They have forsaken me,

the spring of living water,

and have dug their own cisterns,

broken cisterns that can't hold water.

Several years ago, the Lord confronted me to reach out to a young man that had surrendered his life to Christ that had repented of the sins of his former lifestyle. It was tragic witnessing his backsliding as the Lord gave me no choice but to call to meet with him. When I picked him up, we went to a McDonald's and it was obvious that he knew why we were meeting. We finally found a table in this crowded place, when the incredible happened as God sent a messenger.

As I lovingly confronted him, he got angry and very defensive saying, "God loves me any way!" At this point, I went silent. Suddenly, this huge black man with skin like a baby appeared out of nowhere, and there is no way he was hearing this confrontation. He leaned over into the face of my friend, and said, "Remember Sodom and Gomorrah." In amazement and passion, I responded with, "Better yet, remember Lot's wife." When I looked back to respond to this messenger, he had literally vanished. My friend looked at me with tears grabbing and shaking the table and said, "Oh my God, not in a McDonald's!?" He then pleaded for me to take him back home. He left town quickly and I still have him on my heart.

Addressing apostasy, whether moral or spiritual is as uncomfortable as confronting someone you love that is having an affair. It is difficult handling a two-edged sword. We have we reached the place where Jude warned us to "be merciful to those who doubt; save others by snatching them from the fire; to others show mercy, mixed with fear, hating even the clothing stained by corrupted flesh. There will be no turning back.

Looking back to the nineteenth century, the French author, Alexis de Tocqueville, best known for his book, "Democracy in America," came and deeply searched here for the heart of the "greatness of America." After investigating our government, education, commerce, and other entities, he found the answer. He eventually received the revelation that it was not until "he witnessed the flames coming from the pulpit of the churches, that he truly understood."

Today, who will speak the uncomfortable flaming truth to our nation? As Jeremiah, we are now learning with increasing painful realization what we can expect to go through in these final years of our nation's collapse? The answer will certainly will not come from the pulpits of the presiding pillow prophets of the nominal church or the deceitful politicians selling their wares in our capital. In fact, they are the veiled cankerworms at the root. As the remnant is finding their way home with no compromise, they will be the witnesses at the door of the rapture. The "restrainer" is already in place standing in the gap against the global tide. If we don't resist the lawless apostasy, who will?

Our First Sifting Exodus from Europe

2 Chronicles 5

If my people, who are called by my name, will humble themselves and pray and seek my face and turn from their wicked ways, then I will hear from heaven, and I will forgive their sin and will heal their land. Now my eyes will be open and my ears attentive to the prayers offered in this place. I have chosen and consecrated this temple so that my Name may be there forever. My eyes and my heart will always be there.

Unlike Israel, the birth of our nation was not a direct conception from God, yet it was definitely conceived in a prophetic way with a "new exodus." We were not declared as a theocracy as the nation of Israel, but we were founded on the Judeo-Christian foundation. We were based on "freedom of religion, not on freedom from religion." You have the right to travel any road freely, but realize there will be a toll booth at the end of the road.

As a faithful remnant in our nation, we are traveling the road of secular persecution being paved by those hijacking the nation for selfish pleasure and a cancel culture. The sifted pioneers had to suffer the same perils of persecution and seduction from the European church and state before they were baptized through the ocean. Our nation began its journey, graced from the beginning exodus to become a beacon of Light to the falling nations as they escaped from their tyranny. Our forefathers of faith chose to be under the graceful hand of God rather than the hand of worldly kings and the nominal state churches.

The dissention against the state church and the falling state began to swell. The Magna Carta was written in 1215 that was to limit the power of the English king. It even remains important today as a symbol of protest against the authoritarianism progressing from Washington D.C. The Magna Carta was transformed into our beautiful Constitution to repel the empty promises of the taskmasters. Yet, at the writing of the Constitution, there was a "fly in the ointment." There was a dispute over "the pursuit of happiness" versus the "pursuit of holiness." Sadly, the leaven of "the pursuit of happiness" from the remnant of godless Deists began to take root from that point forward.

The cauldron of humanism eventually dwarfed into the Age of Enlightenment that was also called the Age of Reason. It became a large swamp in the eighteenth-century, riddled with mysticism, religion, and the superstitions from the Middle Ages. The Age of Reason represented a twisted perception in the way man viewed himself, the pursuit of knowledge, and the universe. It returned mankind to assuming he was the reason for his brightness that was derived from Lucifer. Reason, rationality and self-enlightenment returned and was touted as the "new gods" from Babylonian roots. This was the beginning of a society where individuals were encouraged to pursue their individual happiness over the true liberty by the Holy Spirit with no fear of retribution.

The decay of spiritual and cultural relativism has re-infested Europe and has invaded our nation through the globalist agenda. The implosion of faith in European young people is staggering and it has followed its way here to ours. Churches in Europe have converted into bars and restaurants as faith has left the building. Prayer and repentance have made way for drinking and dancing in the vacated buildings before the golden calf of Egypt.

As with the nation of Israel, it is impossible to separate the spiritual content of the witness for God from the nation itself. But we have learned historically that theocracy has been used as a trap by the prince of this world. We have to look at the church and state together, as Israel did. Today, some vehemently disagree that our nation originally was "one nation under God." That has what has brought us to be "one nation under the judgement of God." Our foundation was absolutely founded on Judeo-Christian values but with the freedom of choice. Our constitution mandates that we have freedom of religion, not freedom from religion.

In the Book of Matthew, Jesus finally through down the gauntlet for both the pharisees and the Romans and he knew what the price would be. The declaration of the "Seven Woes" emphatically declared who we are facing today. We have come to the same fork in the road where you must decide who you will serve. It is more complicated today because the questions are even more complicated. Are you a believer willing to die for your Master? Are you also a true patriot willing to die for the nation under the assault by "wolves in sheep's clothing? If you do not choose, then they will choose for you.

Our Present Sifting Exodus into Adultery

Job 31

I made a covenant with my eyes not to look lustfully at a young woman. For what is our lot from God above, our heritage from the Almighty on high? Is it not ruin for the wicked, disaster for those who do wrong?

"There is not a single important cultural, religious, political or social force that is pulling Americans together more than it is pushing us apart."

Since the road from the Tower of Babel, humanity has been trying to reunify under the same banner that provoked the flood. The LORD solemnly warned, "If as one people speaking the same language, they have begun to do this, then nothing they plan to do will be impossible for them." The Lord then scattered them by sifting them through their language and communication. In today's final prophetic Babylon, will there be a reprieve for us or have we reached the point of no return. Satan has enacted his webbed "systematized error" to unify the lawless rebels as the Lord is sifting the globe with a differing method of separation.

This blaring topic is the source of my greatest agony in writing this book. I had to address this same trauma before in my last book, "In the Valley of Decision." The heart of the book exposes the fatal flaw in one of my greatest heroes, King David. It also exposes that our nation is intricately mirroring and following the same path of the cataclysmic sin of David as our eyes deceive us. When King David retired from battle he was left to his own devices. This addresses what happens when you are in the good times and your faith is choked when your eyes betray you. This is what happened to us after World War Two. The betrayal of King David went from apathy to temptation to adultery to murder to cover his fatal sin. His betrayal eventually cratered the nation of Israel. Solemnly, we are deep into the same path with far greater consequences from the debacle of "selfism." This truly summarizes the short saying, "the truth hurts."

The legs on which are republic has always stood are the Word of God and our inspired Constitution. Yet, we have slowly abandoned the foundation of prayer and devotion to a complete and total rebellion in just a few generations. We are now wobbling as a drunkard from deferring to the toxic cup of "selfism" because we want what we want, not what we need. We have become the prey to lawlessness as we fall as every empire before us for the very same reasons.

The phrase "playing the harlot" has its roots in ancient times and has been used in various contexts throughout history, especially with Israel. It is one of the terms used to describe apostasy in the Bible. A harlot is defined as a prostitute, a woman who engages in casual sexual encounters or relationship for her own gain. In the Bible, "playing the harlot" describes spiritual prostitution in which the people forsake God and offer their acts of worship, prayer, and sacrifice to other idols, especially self. This "planned deception" is nothing new, it is just final.

Here are some of the contaminants of the sorcery in the cup of lawlessness that continue to intoxicate the nation.

The Sifting Sorcery of Selfism

Luke 9

Then he said to them all: "Whoever wants to be my disciple must deny themselves and take up their cross daily and follow me.

The greatest sin and impact upon the nation and the present global arena is the tsunami of "selfism." This was conceived as Eve was instructed that the Lord was holding them from personal godhood. The cornerstone of all of carnal delusion today is founded in the lethal carnal paradigm shift from betraying God.

As we have covered, the lie of the serpent was the seduction that you could be a "god" from sensual hedonism. We now dwell in the fruition of this carnival of pleasure and pain, with self on the throne. This new wave of permissiveness entailed the morphing changes in morals and a returning spiritual decadence. It was labeled as a new freedom of openness in personal relations and modes of expression with no boundaries. It was actually rooted long ago when Gnostics assert that all spiritual knowledge is good. Secondly, Gnostics claim to possess an elevated knowledge, a "higher truth" known only to an elite few. Gnosticism comes from the Greek word "gnosis," that means "to know." Gnostics claim to possess a higher knowledge, alien from the Bible, but acquired on some mystical higher plane of existence. The global agenda is permeated with this cancer. It installs the ideology that a small group of elitists deserve to enslave the masses through political, spiritual and economic control.

The Sifting Lie of Relativism

Romans 8

Now if we are children, then we are heirs, heirs of God and co-heirs with Christ, if indeed we.

Today, we are suffering from having no knowledge of the truth that can set us free. It has been replaced with, "all roads lead to God." Perception is embedded the lie that truth with no boundaries. It is the denial of absolute truth, leading to a moral license and a denial of even the existence of sin or God.

Jude initially warned us, "I felt compelled to write and urge you to contend for the faith that was once for all entrusted to God's holy people. For certain individuals whose condemnation was written about[b] long ago have secretly slipped in among you. They are ungodly people, who pervert the grace of our God into a license for immorality and deny Jesus Christ our only Sovereign and Lord.

This stated that truth is absolute with no variation or opinion. The deception of relativism has poisoned the culture again. This revealed that no system of "so-called truth" is more valid than another, and there is no objective standard for truth. When Pilate questioned Jesus with "what is truth?" he gave him an unexpected and unsolvable riddle. Yet, Jesus answered, "You say that I am a king. In fact, the reason I was born and came into the world is to testify to the truth. The tragic truth is we have an avalanche of godless cultural elites that have invaded every level of education and government with the proverb, "There is a way that appears to be right in his own eyes, but in the end, it leads to death.

It is a central heresy of our culture to say that all truth is relative; that one thing may be true for me and quite another may be true for you. This absurdity destroys the very notion of truth, and is the result of distorted thinking. If relativism is true, nothing can be condemned. This has led to "lying" becoming our native language.

Our Sifting Tribalism

1 Corinthians 1

Is Christ divided? Was Paul crucified for you? Were you baptized in the name of Paul? I thank God that I did not baptize any of you except Crispus and Gaius, [15] *so no one can say that you were baptized in my name. (Yes, I also baptized the household of Stephanas; beyond that, I don't remember if I baptized anyone else.) For Christ did not send me to baptize, but to preach the gospel—not with wisdom and eloquence, lest the cross of Christ be emptied of its power.*

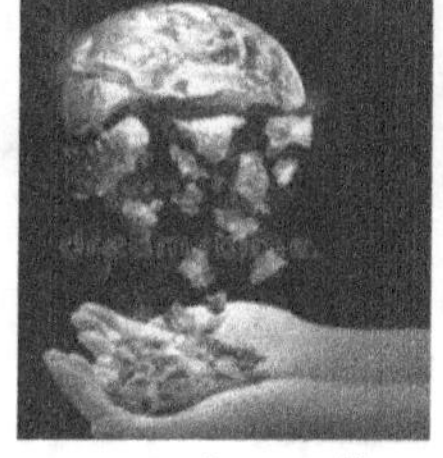

Another severely paralyzing impact on the nation and the planet is the tsunami of tribalism. During the early years of social movements, people would bond together to fight for their rights in ways that make them feel like a tribe fighting for their survival. Our ancestors' bonding was to survive but the shift is about conquering harsh elements and other competing tribes. It was once based on survival, but now it has its basis in annihilation and spiritual cannibalism.

Of all of the birth pains prophesied by Jesus, that have paralyzed the flow of God's will in this nation is five words; nation will rise against nation." The word "nation" in the Greek (ethnos) is the article "ethnic" defining culture, not nations. An ethnicity or ethnic group is a group of people having the same identity on the basis of perceived shared attributes. It is an extension of relativism. There are many places to put the blame from social media, gangs, racial culting, to political parties.

The problems from technology have gotten far worse in the past decade, with social media creating an outrage machine. We received being tribal, but sometimes it's more about the source and the motive. The worst type of tribalism is groups aligned to destroy other groups, such as through ethnic cleansing and genocide. The exploding return of "antisemitism" is a tragic example. Bad tribalism is a group identity that fosters bullying and scapegoating of others different than you. Tribalism expands by the perception that the world around you is out to get you. Unfortunately, tribalism also assumes everyone outside the tribe is your enemy. There is now a "splintering" even within tribes.

The Sifting Mystery of Lawlessness

1 John 3

Everyone who sins breaks the law; in fact, sin is lawlessness. But you know that he appeared so that he might take away our sins. And in him is no sin.

The pedestal of the mystery of lawlessness is now at a fever pitch as we see basic moral standards as faith crashes to the ground. Jesus warned that the persecution from the lies and lawless practices of this era would even corrupt believers. We are now witnessing Christ's solemn question, "when the Son of Man comes, will he find faith on the earth?"

The dark Mystery of Lawlessness is now rampant in our nation, residing in the Harlot's cup of lethal philosophies. The central beliefs of Christianity are in direct opposition to Rome's idolatry and Greek philosophy from men like Socrates, Plato, and Aristotle. On the other hand, it is also true that Christianity was born into a world steeped in Greek thinking. Greek philosophy provided the early Christian church with a vulgar opposition, as well as a persecuting worldview to extinguish the gospel.

Today, the satanic bible's mantra is, "do what you will." The new age delusion's mantra is, "create your own reality." These appear polarized but they are a mirrored deception. The false Luciferian light and the darkness are married influencing what this age stands upon. The legs of the Mystery of Lawlessness are unspeakable rebellion and unbridled apostasy in the name of "selfism. It is impossible to underestimate the gravity of what we are facing. God warns us that to whom much is given, much is required.

Postmodernism follows most of these same deceptions at the end of the century, rejecting previous boundaries and the ancient paths of our forefathers. The basis of truth which held the fabric of social and spiritual order has been disbanded for old philosophies with new labels. It is the continuance of modernism except even more radical. This movement has brought us into a post Christian era in the United States. It has no boundaries and concedes to the posture of relativism which darkens the mind into the abyss.

Facing the Terror in Our Nation Today

Then the word of the LORD came to me. He said, "Can I not do with you, Israel, as this potter does?" declares the LORD. "Like clay in the hand of the potter, so are you in my hand, Israel. If at any time I announce that a nation or kingdom is to be uprooted, torn down and destroyed, and if that nation I warned repents of its evil, then I will relent and not inflict on it the disaster I had planned.

King Solomon declared repeatedly, "there is no new thing under the sun." What has happened to our nation is nothing but a reprint of Satan's scheme from the beginning from empire to empire. The Bible testifies it as well as human history. Daniel's warnings of the coming empires that would fall are precise down to what we are imprisoned in at this moment. The fourth empire prophesied by Daniel was Roman empire. In 750 B.C. the Roman Republic was expanding its political and military control over a vast region in perpetual expansion.

As the empire grew more and more authoritarian, the Caesars found that to maintain control and conceal their escalating corruption, they must indulge the people by distracting them with lies and giving them what wanted. What they didn't understand is they were creating the crumbling of Rome from within. They fed their personal rebellion while closing their iron fist on them.

Our nation and the global facade is facing a reboot of all of the previous empires and cultures by installing the original ploy of "wickedness upon the human race so that every inclination of the thoughts of the human heart was only evil all the time. The Lord's deep regret has returned as "the wrath of God is being revealed from heaven against all the godlessness and wickedness of people, who suppress the truth by their wickedness, as they have clearly seen, and understood so that people are without excuse."

Our nation is repaving this same road with indulgence and ignorance. The Roman empire became more dependent on twisted welfare, as each new Caesar found a way to provide greater and more spectacular orgies and sorceries of every kind. This brought in the new status that an individual's wealth was the number of their idols. The most applicable prescription of the indictment of our nation is found explicitly in the first chapter of the Book of Romans.

Here is a catalog from Romans One of the histories that we are repeating.

Repeating History
Our nation is no longer a "nation under God," but as Rome we are a "nation under the judgment of God."

The Darkening Occult Blindness Suppressing the Truth
Rome suppressed everything from God to the point their Caesars proclaimed to be God as will the coming Antichrist. Moral and spiritual truth was bankrupt and as the Book of Proverbs confesses, "what seems right to a man in his own eyes leads him to death.

Reaping a Corporate and Individual Darkened Heart
The Roman Empire was a primarily polytheistic civilization, which meant that people recognized and worshiped multiple gods and goddesses.

Total Lawlessness through Continually Ignoring God
Through freedom of choice, God will give them over to sinful desires of our hearts to sexual impurity for the degrading of their bodies with one another.

Repeating the History of Rome.
Our government, our educational system, our media, and our technology have paved the way for the "selfism" that has become a new gospel.

> **Becoming Beasts with the Depraved Mind of Relativism**
> *Carnal perception enslaves us to our own evil desires that not only gives birth to sin, it creates settled rebellion of fulfilling every craving of our flesh.*
>
> **Rampant Idolatry from Technology & Earth Worship**
> *Of all of the gods of Rome and Greece, none held more influence as the great mother goddess, Gaia. She was known famously as Mother Earth and climate culture.*
>
> **Rejecting the existence of Sin**
> *The initial sin of pride seared the conscience of Rome. They were mainly concerned with pleasing their gods and their flesh as they were riddled with sin and indulgence from their master.*
>
> **Applauding Others for Doing Even Worse**
> *As they expounded hellish sins and praised ungodliness in culture with maddening new potions, they applauded even deeper sin and praised those who excelled in it.*

The greatest threat in our nation's history was the fracture of the Civil War. From tribal faction from evil slavery, we began crumbling from within. The saying, "War is hell" "is a phrase attributed to the Civil War general, William Sherman. By the end of the war, Sherman had come to believe that the Union's victory required not only defeating the Southern armies, but also destroying the South's physical ability and psychological will to continue the battle.

We are now in the midst of a final "Un-Civil War" politically and spiritually that is splitting us apart as a nation, even down to the soul of the family. Tribalism has taken us barreling toward a cliff of extinction, in word and in deed. Without true repentance, relevant and revelatory, this Civil War as the sky is parted with the coming rapture at the point of no return.

No matter what your political leaning is, most of us can sense that America is barreling toward a cliff of one kind or another. Relevant and revelatory, the next internal Civil War will end in the Valley of Decision. Your decision is being made today because tomorrow will be the door closing.

Facing the Fire

By the grace God has given me, I laid a foundation as a wise builder, and someone else is building it. But each one should build with care. For no one can lay any foundation other than the one already laid, which is Jesus Christ. [12] If anyone builds on this foundation using gold, silver, costly stones, wood, hay or straw, their work will be shown for what it is, because the Day will bring it to light. It will be revealed with fire, and the fire will test the quality of each person's work. If what has been built survives, the builder will receive a reward. If it is burned up, the builder will suffer loss but yet will be saved, even though only as one escaping through the flames.

Although our salvation is eternally secure, the next step of faith is being tried by the fire that is sifting us. There is no "get out of hell free card." We will all stand before the judgment seat of Christ to give an account for the fruit from our branch, not for our forgiveness. If we have surrendered to Christ, the Apostle Paul tells us to be careful how we build on that foundation and that the content of our life is with what can endure the fire. The question is what will be the source of our faith and what will be the source of the fire. When we ask why God tests us or allows us to be tested, we are confessing that it indeed comes from Him. If we neglect Him, the source is the evil one that will consume us. When God tests His children, He does an invaluable thing of bringing genuineness to our faith. When the fire comes from the world, it sifts and separates us from God.

Earlier, we saw how Abraham was tested by God in the matter of sacrificing Isaac, he obeyed and proved that he is the father of faith. Without that test, there would be no Israel. Later, David sought God's testing, by asking Him to examine his heart and mind to see that they were true to Him. When God tests His children, His purpose is to test the quality of their faith through purification to holiness. He is proving to us that we are truly His children, and that no trial will overcome our faith if we embrace it. Fire is the agent of change for sacrifice, purification or annihilation. It is the sifting vehicle to temper our natural man into God's image or to transfer us to perish in the flames. We do not favor anyone by tampering with the Lord's eternal process of true redemption.

In the last book of the Old Testament, the prophet Malachi sums up this purpose by saying, "He will sit as a refiner and purifier of silver, and he will purify the sons of Levi and refine them like gold and silver, and they will bring offerings in righteousness to the LORD." Malachi names the Lord "the Sun of righteousness" with healing in His wings. To the remnant, the Messiah burning in spirit is the blade of surgical construction., not destruction. When are compelled to embrace the truth, we to produce eternal fruit that sets us free from this world and from ourselves.

Facing the Whole Truth

John 3

For God so loved the world that he gave his one and only Son, that whoever believes in him shall not perish but have eternal life. For God did not send his Son into the world to condemn the world, but to save the world through him. Whoever believes in him is not condemned, but whoever does not believe stands condemned already because they have not believed in the name of God's one and only Son. This is the verdict: Light has come into the world, but people loved darkness instead of light because their deeds were evil. Everyone who does evil hates the light, and will not come into the light for fear that their deeds will be exposed. But whoever lives by the truth comes into the light, so that it may be seen plainly that what they have done has been done in the sight of God.

If you tell the truth, you don't have to remember anything. Mark Twain

What is the "whole truth" concerning the nation? The whole truth is we love what we embrace and ingest. When we have chosen to not reject sin as it devours us, we have chosen to remove God and reject Him. It has tragically been done in our schools, in our government, and in our culture to the point His Spirit is even being sifted from the nominal church. Jesus warned us, "a little leaven will leaven the whole loaf."

The scripture John 3:16 is the most notorious scripture in the New Testament, but it is incomplete without the continuing verses that are kept silent. They are never quoted because they are the verdict; the whole truth concerning "unbelief." The Bible is not to be a cafeteria where you choose your favorites. It is to be an instrument of "sifting" and a two-edged sword to separate our soul from our spirit. It lays bare all things, all vows, and all lies.

Tragically, a heart that has already been compromised is in heart failure, not valid for surgery. We are perishing as a nation as Bibles clutter our bookshelves in dust and we starve spiritually.

Mass media has slowly become the hemlock we drink since the technology birthed from the last world war. Now, Hollywood and television have now even been eclipsed by social media. I love Generation Z, but they are prodigal orphans left to feed from the scraps of a fallen society. They are being consumed by consuming what the pigs have left. It has morphed their appetite for truth into lawlessness and compromise. In reality, our foundation of freedom of choice has gone from our greatest blessing to our greatest curse.

In the Book of Matthew, Jesus cautioned against the practice of making shallow, compromised, and careless oaths. Christ has called us to a life of truthfulness, integrity, and sincerity before Him and all people. Sadly, "so help me God" has even become another reckless oath on the lips of many who often spout it as an angry threat. Do we stand as one nation under God, saying, so help me God or saying leave me alone. The very worst choice is compromise. James warned us that a double-minded man can expect to receive nothing from God. That is our dilemma as a nation today.

If you continue to choose to stand in the middle it will soon sift you in two; soul and body. Not only can a house divided not stand, neither can a nation, and neither can you. You can't serve two masters and you can't travel two roads at the same time. Jesus taught there are only two roads, the broad and the narrow. Christ concluded the Sermon on the Mount by telling the people they had to choose one way or the other. Either the narrow road to the kingdom of heaven that leads to life or the broad road of this world leading to destruction.

CHAPTER SEVEN
The Current Sifting of the Church

2 Timothy 4

In the presence of God and of Christ Jesus, who will judge the living and the dead, and in view of his appearing and his kingdom, I give you this charge: Preach the word; be prepared in season and out of season; correct, rebuke and encourage—with great patience and careful instruction. For the time will come when people will not put up with sound doctrine. Instead, to suit their own desires, they will gather around them a great number of teachers to say what their itching ears want to hear. [4] *They will turn their ears away from the truth and turn aside to myths.*

In the beginning the church was a fellowship of men and women centered on the living Christ. Then the church moved to Greece, where it became a philosophy. Then it moved to Rome, where it became an institution. Next, it moved to Europe, where it became **a** culture. And, finally, it moved to America, where it became an enterprise."
Richard Halverson, former chaplain of the United States Senate

The above quote is an ominous indictment of the presiding nominal church in our nation and the globe. It is a concise and sobering truth on how the devices of persecution and seduction were weaponized by the prince of this world to sift the church from any value at the end of church age. In the Book of Revelation, the Apostle John was astonished by the betrayal of the mysterious Harlot riding on the Beast. I am now astonished and weeping over what has happened to the nominal church as it ventured out of the torrential current of the Sixties into the arena of the "grazing Maze."

In beautiful sacrifice, the virgin church arose from the veins of our Messiah and was extended through the blood and the Spirit of the first church at Pentecost. For the following two centuries, the church of God was literally bathed in blood. Thousands of believers were tortured and murdered in the most inhumane way. Though the atrocities of this period were horrific, the persecutions launched an unquenchable revival that continued in the coliseums of Rome. The suffering and hardships tempered those who were truly converted to Jesus. It sifted out much of the hypocritical element which was already starting to plague the church.

What is the mission taking place in the church today? As we now are witnessing the door closing to the church age, what are we doing to stem the tide of apostasy? The heavens are appalled as we continue to sow among the thorns. For the "nominal Christian, this will not end well as the "Thief of heaven" removes the precious remnant and robs the graves of the sleeping saints. This will be the final sifting of the last nominal church, and as I mentioned before, "nominal" means in name only.

According to CRC Director of Research Dr. George Barna, American Christianity is now undergoing a "post-Christian Reformation, and rather than providing leadership and faithfulness in an age of moral decline, members of the majority of the nation's major Christian groups are rapidly leaving biblical foundations behind and exchanging traditional theological beliefs for the culture's secular values." How agonizing it is to witness the last stage of the fall of the historic church to an "enterprise." We are now drowning in the merchandising that the Apostle Paul warned the church in Corinth about. The nominal church had taken its seat and was thriving in their midst. Paul challenged them by saying, "Unlike so many, we do not peddle the word of God for profit. On the contrary, in Christ we speak before God with sincerity, as those sent from God."

But as only the Apostle Paul could do by speaking the truth in love, this was the following address to this compromised church. "But thanks be to God, who always leads us as captives in Christ's triumphal procession and uses us to spread the aroma of the knowledge of him everywhere. For we are to God the pleasing aroma of Christ among those who are being saved and those who are perishing. To the one we are an aroma that brings death; to the other, an aroma that brings life. And who is equal to such a task?" So, how have we arrived at this fatal point is defined in our final generation of "forgetting our first love."

The Mystery of Lawlessness seeded in the Sixties led us to a new crisis of identity as the first "Me" generation which even began to leaven the nominal church. A river of self-centered teachings for profit led to spiritual anarchy never seen before. The blade of the Messiah began to expose and sift the apostates through scandal. Some fell to their knees but many continue even now living in their mansions as they bleed out the local church.

The seeding age of televangelism helped morph the nominal church into Christian theater and set the stage for the complicit return of the duplicity and lawlessness practiced by the Pharisees. The critical line has been drawn with the use of lawlessness being exchanged for the crippling previous legalism. For the most part, it has fermented into a belly button theology of "selfism" as a multi-billion-dollar business. Today, we have also exchanged the healing savor of salt, replacing it with the taste of sugar.

This has brought us through the doors of the final prophetic church age to the lukewarm nominal church of Laodicea. Their mantra was, "I am rich; I have acquired wealth and do not need a thing." Then Jesus replied, "But you do not realize that you are wretched, pitiful, poor, blind and naked. I counsel you to buy from me gold refined in the fire, so you can become rich; and white clothes to wear, so you can cover your shameful nakedness; and salve to put on your eyes, so you can see."

The irony is the fact that they thought they were perfect, but they were truly blind even to their own condition. The greatest sin here was that they had stopped listening and that they were in love with the sound of their own voice. They had not only shut the door to repentance, but they were playing the harlot to the world. They had the attributes of the unbelievers around them far more than the faith.

The rebuke to this church is profound and it is not only last in sequence, it is last in devotion and character. Jesus speaks the words of the Amen, the faithful and true witness to this final church in Laodicea, and us today that, has fallen to apathy and apostasy. To the church in Laodicea in their lukewarm, indifferent, self-sufficient attitude, the Lord presents Himself as "the Amen, the faithful and true witness." This church has forsaken her heavenly calling and settled for her own resources and comfort.

In summary, we are also now sharing the unbelief that fell on the children of Israel in their falling short of the Promised Land. They tested the Lord as He should have been testing them while they murmured and whined that they would have rather stayed as slaves in Egypt. God had delivered them constantly, even from the Egyptian army in the Red Sea as he drowned them as they were delivered. Their hearts were always astray and they never learned who He truly was. This great sin of having a rampant heart of unbelief has leavened the present witness of the nominal church. I

I Never Knew You

Matthew 7

"Not everyone who says to me, 'Lord, Lord,' will enter the kingdom of heaven, but only the one who does the will of my Father who is in heaven. Many will say to me on that day, 'Lord, Lord, did we not prophesy in your name and in your name drive out demons and, in your name, perform many miracles?' Then I will tell them plainly, 'I never knew you. Away from me, you who practice lawlessness!

The Apostle Paul was already witnessing the Mystery of Lawlessness invading his present evil age that was also fermenting the church in his hour. The scriptures above end with an emphatic warning to those who practice lawlessness by merchandising in the name of Jesus. The practice of "merchandising" is a great sin and a brutal sign of what owns you. This eerily links to the love of most growing cold from the final apostate rebellion leading to the Antichrist. This warning comes at the conclusion of the incredible Sermon on the Mount. It clenches the nail of what and who is a true disciple.

In the beginning of Christ's mission, Jesus went into the Temple after braiding a whip, as he began to cleanse the Temple of the merchandising hypocrites. He said, "Get these out of here!

Stop turning my father's house into a market and a den of thieves!" As His first revelation as the Messianic King, He began sifting the Judaic apostasy that would lead to their Diaspora. They proclaimed they wanted the Messiah to rescue them from Rome, but they rejected their Savior and Lord. This spiritual leaven found its way quickly into a peripheral clan claiming to be disciples.

The sifting of the church began when Jesus harshly replied, "I never knew you" to these present disciples of duplicity who had already started their own merchandising. Jesus had to expose their true hearts before they leavened the whole lump. He expressed that He never truly knew them as His intimate disciples or His friends. He never had any connection with them nor did He approve of them, because they were thieves. They had no relationship with Him, but they were selling wares that they had stolen.

Christ did not have a place in their hearts, nor did they have Him in mind. Understand that Jesus is not breaking off the relationship here, there was never a true relationship to break off. The word in Greek "ginoskow" for the word "knowing" was the same word used concerning the intimate relationship with a husband and wife. So, what really mattered isn't so much that they knew God on some level, but that God truly did not know them, just as we can know His Word without it knowing us.

Who Are These Merchants Today?

Matthew 25

"At that time the kingdom of heaven will be like ten virgins who took their lamps and went out to meet the bridegroom. Five of them were foolish and five were wise. The foolish ones took their lamps but did not take any oil with them. The wise ones, however, took oil in jars along with their lamps.

"There are two kinds of people: those who say to God, 'Thy will be done,' and those to whom God says, 'All right then, have it your way."   C.S. Lewis

We will now focus on the extreme revelations in the parables of Christ for this closing hour. We will be covering the parable of the Ten Virgins in detail later, but there is a plethora of truths revealed in this parable that are very significant concerning these compromising merchants. This parable extends to many questions and many answers. The basic warning of Jesus in this specific parable was the participants are all virgins (believers) yet they are sifted by wisdom and foolishness, having no oil in their vessels, just pretension. The other key is where do the foolish virgins go as the door is shut when the Bridegroom comes and retrieves the wise. The severe question we must ask is "will there be professing Christians who will be stunned to witness that they were not taken in the rapture?" This is a hidden key to the door of the kingdom.

This defines something deeper between the splitting of the church at the arrival of the Bridegroom and King. The are two streams flowing in this hour being divided into two cisterns of the church. There is one streaming from the counterfeit Mystery of Lawlessness as the other is streaming within the souls of the committed remnant separating them by the mystery of godliness. In each case, the "mystery" involves a declaration of spiritual sifting revealed by God through divine inspiration. The Greek word translated "godliness" means "a proper response to the things of God, which produces obedience and righteous living." The mystery of godliness is at the very heart of the Christian faith. The Apostle Paul told Timothy that, "Beyond all question, the mystery from which true godliness springs is great." This brings us to choose whether to sell out to Babylon, the Great or the humility of the cross.

The indictment of these merchants led to their expulsion for what they had not purchased. Thus, in the present context, it denotes the current apostasy from the faith. Paul tells us specifically what this "unrighteous deception" is for which the people become deserters of the faith. He names the "Mystery of Lawlessness," as a set of beliefs that are totally contrary to the truth and based on self-determination. This deception is the fruit of the Great Lie" since the garden of Eden. It is the alliance with evil extorting from God and becoming the "enemies of the cross." After Jesus had harshly warned, "I never knew you," to these presiding disciples of duplicity, he spoke that their fate was sealed, but was it an eternal fate?

We will now peer into some of the parables on this topic. It is amazing that approximately one third of Christ's teachings were parables. Parables are told in an historical context that draws on culture, historical events, and specific timeframes. We need to always know what the historical and cultural contexts are. Each parable has a heart and soul message with a distinct direction. If you don't understand the question, you can't come up with the right answer. The central message of many parables was about being ready for the kingdom of God at Christ's return. This is not the time to be asleep at the wheel. We need to focus on the many specific parables that give a grave warning to redeem the time and not to put off the Day of Evil.

The Parable of the Wedding Feast

Matthew 22

Then he said to his servants, 'The wedding is ready, but those who were invited were not worthy. Therefore, go into the highways, and as many as you find, invite to the wedding.' So those servants went out into the highways and gathered together all whom they found, both bad and good. And the wedding hall was filled with guests. "But when the king came in to see the guests, he saw a man there who did not have on a wedding garment. So, he said to him, 'Friend, how did you come in here without a wedding garment?' And he was speechless. Then the king said to the servants, 'Bind him hand and foot, take him away, and cast him into outer darkness; there will be weeping and gnashing of teeth.' "For many are called, but few are chosen."

This parable is in the context of the Lord's Passion Week in which Jesus was betrayed and crucified. It condemns the horrid contempt that Israel's betrayal of God's gracious invitation through Jesus, their Messiah. This parable once again contained a veiled judgment on the self-righteous Jews that came not to receive their King but to cause Him to stumble. If they could discredit him, they could keep the pathetic image of themselves by distorting the law.

This parable was centered on the naked pharisees and now it is exposing the nominal church as being just as complicit today. It speaks to the called people that had been invited, but when the time for the banquet feast came and the table was set, those invited refused to even come with impotent excuses. The true reason they rejected the invitation is that they do not revere the King, because they were caught in "selfism." The inviting king was enraged at the response of those who had been invited, sent his army to avenge the death of his servants. He then sent invitations to those unworthy that were lost in the streets so that the wedding hall would be filled. The humbled on the streets received their entrance, because they are empty and have a desperate need for the truth.

The next focus of the Parable of the Wedding Feast tells of an invited guest that entered the wedding hall unprepared without a wedding garment. It is puzzling that the king was not furious with him as he was with those that refused to even show up. When the king sees him, he calls him, "Friend, how did you come in here without a wedding garment?" The king then says, "Bind him hand and foot and cast him into the outer darkness." The improperly dressed wedding guest had answered the call to the wedding, yet he didn't take it seriously. The king reluctantly dealt with him differently. The parable is clear that those that are called and unprepared will be cast into outer darkness. This parable ends with the mysterious indictment, "For many are called, but few are chosen." This a grave warning to each of is today.

Jesus uses the term "outer darkness" in these parables to describe the condition of great sorrow, loss and woe. It stands in vivid contrast to the brightly lit and joyous celebration attended by those who accepted the king's invitation and prepared for the event. But it is clear this is about outer darkness, not the fire and eternal separation of hell. This is why the Book of Hebrews warns us, "how shall we escape if we ignore so great a salvation? Interpreting the wedding feast as heaven is clear, but is the "outer darkness" actually a place of eternal punishment?

The Parable of the Talents

Matthew 25

For whoever has will be given more, and they will have an abundance. Whoever does not have, even what they have will be taken from them. And throw that worthless servant outside, into the darkness, where there will be weeping and gnashing of teeth.

All of the parables are based on being accountable in sacrifice and service. This parable depicts investing in God's Kingdom to accomplish the Lord's purpose. This is a personal message about living before the Lord and forsaking the kingdom of darkness. From the time of the creation of mankind, each individual has been entrusted with resources of time and material wealth.

Everything we have, comes from God and belongs to Him alone. In Jesus' time, a steward was a manager, not the owner, but a responsible administrator of the owner's property. We are all stewards of the Lord's possessions and influence. Our great responsibility is to be stewards using those resources so that they increase in value and produce fruit. We must understand that we will all give an account, today or tomorrow.

In this parable, the master is the lord of these servants which is a representation of Jesus Himself. He makes it understood that he expects his servants to be responsible and productive. As with the Messiah's return, there is a long delay that tempts the servants to think that they would never give an account for their stewardship, yet they were warned they certainly would. The servants were given different amounts of money according to their ability. One servant only received one talent, yet we should see that this was not an insignificant amount. Some received more; but everyone received a large amount.

The first and second stewards were faithful, and they received a double reward, even though one was given five talents and the other was given two talents. We should carefully note the outcome of faithful service, and of unfaithful service, in this parable. Faithful service led to increased responsibilities in the kingdom of heaven, and eternal joy in the presence of the Master, Jesus Christ with great reward. They both use the resources by "trading" to gain a profit for their Master, not for themselves. Each of these servants makes a one hundred percent profit.

The master's dealings with the third servant are a very different matter. This servant came to his master with the talent his master had originally entrusted to him. He did not invest his master's money at all. This servant offered a feeble excuse for his conduct when he buried it in the ground. He told his master that he was harsh and cruel, a man who was demanding, and who expected gain where he had not labored. In reality, he blamed his master. He contended that this is why he was afraid to take a risk with any kind of investment. So, he simply hid the money, and now he returned it, without any gain. He excused himself by claiming that fear and mistrust of his Lord motivated him. This is a direct indictment of today's nominal believer.

The master rebuked this servant for being evil and lazy. The untrusting steward is scolded, rejected, and then punished. He took his talent from him, gave it to the one who earned much, and cast this fellow into outer darkness, where there was weeping and gnashing of teeth. This "weeping" describes an inner pain of the heart, mind, and spirit. The word in the original denotes a bewailing or lamentation by beating the breast in an expression of immense sorrow.

This worthless servant will face the Judgment Seat of Christ with the other two servants who were rewarded as faithful. Are unbelievers given a stewardship by the Lord? The parable shows that the third servant knows the Lord, but uncompliant. He knew the Lord would hold him accountable. He responds by doing nothing, evidently thinking he is taking the safe route, but the idea that he does not know the Lord is contrary to the passage. The most natural explanation of these texts is that outer darkness is a figure for shame and sadness. It refers to a literal place, but it is contrary to Hades or to the lake of fire. In fact, it is the Tribulation.

This parable was first a message to the people of Israel, but now it is an even stronger warning to the nominal church living in the last days before the Lord returns. We are told a key statement, "But he that shall endure unto the end, the same shall be saved." This is a specific call to those during this Day of Evil. This is the believing remnant that will receive the promise of the kingdom that were fruitful. These will be alive when He appears as a "Thief" and will have understood and believed their Lord. The basis of the reward will be their stewardship of His resources entrusted to them.

There is a repeating key to open this mystery that Jesus revealed that is so often misunderstood. He only spoke of "outer darkness" in only three parables which are recorded in the Gospel of Matthew. In these stories, it is certain that outer darkness is a horrid place of sifting and separation. Jesus described a situation in which we would never want to find ourselves, but is this hell? Many theologians hold that the "outer darkness" in these three incidents is literally referencing the fiery hell. Then, how does this reconcile with hell's depiction as a place of eternal, unquenchable fire? If hell is a place of literal darkness, how could it also be a place with literal fire since flames produce light? Is it a fire that has no light?"

This issue has another answer that is also extremely uncomfortable that we will discuss later. Generally, outer darkness has been taught to be hell, however, it is associated more generally as "a place of separation from God, which is assumed to be eternal. Outer darkness is married to the expression of weeping and gnashing of teeth is not a technical expression that refers to hell either. But neither of these judgments are located in hell. It is inescapable, unless some unbelievers that are called servants are judged at the Judgment Seat of Christ, while other are other believers are judged at the Great White Throne Judgment seat. The expression "the sons of the kingdom" only occurs one other time in the Book of Matthew. There, it clearly refers to the faithful. This is an example of why Paul loved the Bereans because they always verified by the scripture.

Being sifted from the nominal church, there is the believing remnant that will receive the full promise of the kingdom that are producing fruit. They will be alive when He returns to extract them at the rapture. The same sifting is occurring now with the people of Israel as they will eventually be rescued in the Valley of Decision. Please understand that this is not about eternal security, it is about accountability. The second death received at the great white throne is eternal damnation for those that reject the blood of Jesus and confess their godless works. This warning here is about the nominal believer suffering loss, but not eternally. As Paul warned, " If what has been built survives, the builder will receive a reward. If it is burned up, the builder will suffer loss but yet will be saved, even though only as one escaping through the flames."

This message doesn't sell well in the nominal church and it is not supposed to. Our repeat of the days of Noah is occurring as Jesus warned, "For in the days before the flood, people were eating and drinking, marrying and giving in marriage, up to the day Noah entered the ark." Also, the return of Sodom was about "buying and selling." The fact is only the truth will set you free. The Apostle Paul verified that the greatest responsibility pf a pastor was to equip his flock for service not just blessing. In this hour, we are "to trust in the Lord and not to lean on our understanding." We must also be careful of who we are leaning on around us. We are warned that even "the very elect of God would be deceived if it were possible."

Rightly Dividing the Word of Truth

2 Timothy 2

Keep reminding God's people of these things. Warn them before God against quarreling about words; it is of no value, and only ruins those who listen. Do your best to present yourself to God as one approved, a worker who does not need to be ashamed and who correctly handles the word of truth.

There is an ancient story of an elephant and a group of blind men who had never come across an elephant before. They tried to learn what the elephant is like by touching it. Then, each blind man felt a different part of the elephant's body, but only one part, such as a leg, a tail or the tusk. They then described the elephant based on their limited experience, but their descriptions of the elephant are totally different from each other. The moral of this story is that humans have a tendency to claim absolute truth based on their limited, subjective experience as they ignore spiritual reality.

The Apostle Paul encouraged Timothy, "to be diligent to present himself as a workman approved by God who would not need to be ashamed because he was rightly dividing or accurately handling the Word of Truth." We must be committed to doing the work defined by scripture and to be equipped for what God intends us to do in life. Secondly, Paul fully understood the total validity in the Word is not about the approval of men but God, and thank God we have the whole "elephant of the Bible today.

There is assurance that this issue that I am opening will sift many and will once again ruffle the feathers of some sincere believers, that reject the whole truth of accountability. This could be the most controversial question of Christian theology. It has led to division between Christians, Catholics, and innumerable others who confess Jesus Christ as their Lord. The question is "are people saved simply through believing in Jesus, yet refusing to be obedient by their works?" This brings us to even a greater barrier of conditional salvation or eternal security. Arminianism explains the relationship between God's sovereignty and humanity's free will in relation to salvation. Yet, Calvinism emphasizes the sovereignty of God, Arminianism emphasizes the responsibility of man. There are valid, sincere believers on both sides with valid support yet not complete. I hope you will understand why I have risked opening this volatile issue. Eternal security professes that anyone who comes to genuine faith in Jesus Christ can never lose their salvation. In the sixth chapter of John, Jesus makes several promises regarding those who follow Him. He shares He will never cast out a believer and He will never lose one that His Father has given, and they will be with Him for eternity.

Conditional security states that a believer in Christ will remain saved based on the condition of having preserved his faith to the end. Armenians give the assurance based on a godly life you are secure if you persevere without apostasy or unbelief. So, conditional security says that our salvation not only depends on the grace of God who gives us faith as preservation, but also the responsibility of the believer to hold onto that preservation and build upon his or her faith.

This stems to the issue of another controversial debate among theologians between severe discipline versus eternal judgment. A grave example of this debacle is when Paul told the Corinthian church what to do with a man caught in incest as one who is present with you in this way, He said, "I have already passed judgment in the name of our Lord Jesus on the one who has been doing this. So, when you are assembled and I am with you in spirit, and the power of our Lord Jesus is present, hand this man over to Satan for the destruction of the flesh, so that his spirit may be saved on the Day of the Lord.

This issue is a mosaic of the truth that is often displayed through integral missing pieces. That is why we are compelled to study the Bible to be approved. The false assurance of convincing someone that they are saved by mouthing a prayer without repentance leaves you outside the door of trusting your life with Christ by His Spirit and the Word. Just as deadly is causing someone to doubt their saving faith by a phobia to sin and magnifying their flaws. Grace and truth are the legs that we must stand upon. This compels us to be active by faith through works because faith without works is dead. Keep your eyes upon the whole elephant.

CHAPTER EIGHT
The Current Sifting of the Nations

1 Thessalonians 5

Now, brothers and sisters, about times and dates we do not need to write to you, for you know very well that the day of the Lord will come like a thief in the night. While people are saying, "Peace and safety," destruction will come on them suddenly, as labor pains on a pregnant woman, and they will not escape.

Revelation 6

I watched as the Lamb opened the first of the seven seals. Then I heard one of the four living creatures say in a voice like thunder, "Come!" I looked, and there before me was a white horse! Its rider held a bow, and he was given a crown, and he rode out as a conqueror bent on conquest.

"We are on the verge of a global transformation. All we need is the right major crisis and the nation will accept the New World Order."
David Rockefeller

The above quote by David Rockefeller, who is just one of the many devout global elitists that are now hell bent on completing what they now term, "The Global Reset." Rockefeller's message was a simple one, "give us control and we will do a much better job of managing things," but the truth is, it is about managing you. The Rockefellers are funding the Islamic terrorists that are invading our universities. They are responsible for dissolving our borders, bankrupting our moral code along with the banking system and fear mongering in the names of things such as "climate change."

The horrid reality is not that they have just invaded our nation, it is they have risen from within it. They not only sit in our banks and our schools; they have captured the capital and the White House at this point. Even worse, just how far will they let the United Nations and their global tentacles go to achieve their control in every crevice of the globe. Forgive my bluntness but they are the rising "Fourth Reich" with a new "Final Solution," far worse than the regime of Adolph Hitler. It is not about the climate, or war or overpopulation, it is about control at any price, especially with what ends up in their pockets. What is so bewildering is these traitors are dismantling our nation, rewriting our history and spending us to death. We are about to reach stage four of this disease while the nominal church passively drinks the "Kool-Aid."

The COVID pandemic induced through China which killed millions of people is the beginning crisis that Rockefeller spoke of that would clinch our submission to a global alliance, but they are just getting started. The purchase by China of the White House in recent years is one of the cankerworms at the root. This pandemic was no accident. It is at the very least been orchestrated by spirits from the bowels of hell, yet just look around you. There are a myriad of threads to these beasts that are not even bashful.

The devilish World Economic Forum at Davos Switzerland, just warned that a new pandemic named "Disease X" may be on the way. At this time, China is working feverishly on a "New COVID that will be one hundred per cent fatal. This will again be weaponized for population control and sifting the any dissidents from the globe.

In collusion with the World Health Organization, also based in Switzerland, they have seized control of international health. This covert agency of the United Nations is enforcing a global mandate from the Covid pandemic to supersede every nation's health policy. This was even sanctioned here by our own president. The COVID pandemic set the stage for the governing process being unified globally for the first time since the Tower of Babel. There is a new pandemic from a campaign of lies and deception that are streaming through every facet of global culture that are filled with enough pleasure to bring an unyielding addiction. I have witnessed the rise of social media capture an entire generation seeking companionship.

My book "The Daze of Noah" also exposes another global organization in Switzerland called CERN. Phantom CERN has had a primary goal to validate and prove the existence of what is called "the Higgs field." This would be a monumental discovery for science and human knowledge, and would open doorways to new knowledge in many so-called disciplines. They have spent billions on what is called the Hadron Collider which is a massive, eighteen-mile track that is supposedly to be a particle smasher in the name of quantum physics. Yet, they claim that in the name of metaphysics, they are studying "atomic glue."

The truth is "the devil is truly in the details." The logo of this vile entity is "three spinning sixes" with a plethora of satanic messages that are laced within. The truth is they are actually trying to create a portal to the next dimension which is the "abyss" that is exposed in the ninth chapter in the Book of Revelation.

At the gate of CERN stands the genderless goddess Shiva in a portal of fire. Shiva holds one of the most prominent roles in Hinduism as the "god of destruction." The name Shiva which means "Destroyer" is named by the Apostle John in this verse. "They had as king over them the angel of the Abyss, whose name in Hebrew is Abadon and in Greek is Apollyon (that is, Destroyer). This is where the spirit of the Beast, "will come up out of the abyss and go into perdition. The Antichrist is a hybrid from the possession where he appears to rise from the dead.

The nightmare of not being able to buy or sell is secretly percolating across the planet. A final link to totalitarian global control is coming with, the unity of the mind, the computer, and the internet. The Federal Reserve is about to enliven a digital currency conspiring with international bankers to implement a central bank delcting all other banks by the CBDC, under the guise of erasing international debt. They are secretly merging "digital currency" which refers to ever monetary transaction will be in purely electronic form that is not physically tangible, like a dollar bill or a coin. It will be accounted for and transferred using online systems. All banks will be centralized, and all transactions will be processed through the phantom "Federal Reserve." The New World Order has been hiding in plain sight from Genesis and now is being detailed by the United Nations in New York City. It is veiled within national institutions like the Council on Foreign Relations, and the U.S. government operatives as fronts for the "international bankers" married to the Federal Reserve. Even worse is even a few of our presidents have hidden behind this curtain of Oz.

The Fruition of the Mysterious Mustard Tree

Luke 13

So, this led Him to say, "What is the kingdom of God like? And to what shall I compare it? It is like a mustard seed, which a man took and planted in his own garden; and it grew and became a tree, and THE BIRDS OF THE SKY FOUND SHELTER and NESTED IN ITS BRANCHES. AMP

The mysterious parable of the Mustard Tree is surely the most misunderstood parable in the scripture. It is so far past the many former interpretations because it is seen far out of its expansive time frame. God's Word is not organized as much as it is a living organism. As it branches from the Way of Cain to the Mystery of Lawlessness, the journey is mapped by the Holy Spirit, not our intellect. I know this will seem stranger than science because it is, but we are just scratching the surface concerning the Day of Evil. The more we think we know, the more we get trapped by our own perceptions. This is why Paul deeply warned us that we must be "sober and alert" preparing for the rapture, because you do not want to be left behind in the torrential current of the headwaters of the Tribulation. We must dwell outside of the box of religion or we will end up being its resident.

There is a conflict that arises when you connect the parable of the Mustard Seed with the parable of the Mustard Tree. In the first century, the mustard seed was a controversial choice for a teaching about faith. The point of using the mustard seed was about its size. Jesus uses this tiny seed to express faith as an "uprooter of mountains," which can accomplish great things if that small amount of faith is placed in our great and mighty God. The faith that we must have has more to do with what kind of faith it is than with how much faith there is. This parable is completely positive and must be separated from the parable of the Mustard Tree. The parable of the Mustard Tree is totally different as it warns us concerning leaven warping the kingdom of heaven.

In the first century, the mustard tree was even more controversial as a teaching about the kingdom of Heaven, because it was an unclean plant, not a tree. The Jews also had strict laws against mixing two kinds of crop in the same field. Mustard seed by its nature, would violate boundaries and start taking over the field. If a gardener did not uproot them from their garden, they would soon not have a garden left to tend. Although this parable is a warning concerning leaven warping the kingdom of heaven, the real culprit is who is lodged in her branches.

The thirteenth chapter of Luke is filled with parables concerning the sifting war within the kingdom of God. The parable of the Mustard Tree is the shortest and the most mysterious parable in the scripture, and actually the most hidden. Immediately, this alarming parable is perplexing because mustard seeds only produce a small shrub, not a massive tree. The traditional explanations skirts this mystery by just describing the story as the wonderful growth and spreading influence of the kingdom of God through the ages. In the light of the context of this parable, "the devil is in the details." This parable is also an exposure and indictment of the corruption and evil from the beginning warring against the existing communal kingdom of God from within.

The timeline of this parable begins with the profound exposure of the fallen angelic "Watchers" from the Days of Noah and their return in the present hour. The history of these fallen Watchers is oblivious to most and a distortion to many. They continue Satan's "Great Lie" from the Garden of Eden and they will have their part in consummating the devastating delusion at the very end of the Great Tribulation. They are released from the abyss to cause their horrific imprint in the final hour Their fingerprints are all over the present age. Satan and his cohorts relish in disguise as they operate within a veil with lying wonders.

In the eighteenth chapter of the Book of Revelation, these same wicked birds are caged and then released by the mysterious Harlot of Babylon. She is defined as becoming "a dwelling place for demons, a dungeon haunted by every unclean spirit, and a prison for every unclean and loathsome bird." These demonic fowl have returned to extend the Way of Cain through the present Mystery of Lawlessness as they nestled in women during the Days of Noah. We have to understand that this encompasses the time from Genesis to the Book of Revelation.

The summary of this parable is Satan caging humanity in deception to displace the kingdom of God as our refuge. These denizens of evil lodge in its branches to counterfeit eternal purpose. There is so much at stake as this generation fades away, just living for the moment. We must empty our hearts of vain deception to receive a heart of conviction to find God's perfect will.

The Day of Evil has come upon us from the original assault of the fallen angels in the Book of Genesis. To understand the ending, you must realize the attachment to the beginning. There are very deep reasons as to why that God had to resort to flooding the earth. We are now gazing at the harvest of the seeds that were sown by the angelic dark hosts to bring the world order under their submission. The same bell of history is now tolling the epic warning for us today as it rang for Noah in his generation eclipsed by the dark and perverted. The closing hours of this present evil age is now the tragic reprint with the same fingerprints. The same violence, rising technology, and corruption that induced humanity's incestuous marriage with these returning dark angels bringing the divorcement from God.

Are You Going to Lose Your Mind?

It also forced all people, great and small, rich and poor, free and slave, to receive a mark on their right hands or on their foreheads, so that they could not buy or sell unless they had the mark, which is the name of the beast or the number of its name. This calls for wisdom. Let the person who has insight calculate the number of the beast, for it is the number of a man. That number is 666.

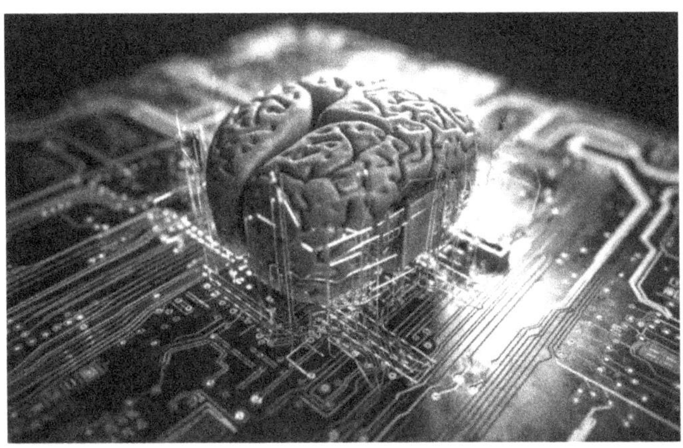

Abbot Saint Bernard of Clairvaux authored, "The road to hell is paved with good intentions." I'm sure he would shudder if he knew how often it has been misapplied. This broad road is paved with anything but good intentions. It is the prince of this world hijacking everything God intended for good. We are told the Antichrist and the False Prophet will come through signs and lying wonders.

I remember well how stunned I was years ago with the intervention of the UPC code as it was bordered with 666. The discovery of the three bordering sixes on the mark made me shiver from the realization that the wolf may be at the door. There has been great speculation for centuries concerning the Mark of the Beast and its identity. It is evident that the Mark of the Beast will be physically and permanently placed on your forehead or right hand. It is numbered by 666, to combines the number of man with the number of God as a fatal mixture. I could never fathom that someone would have any object engraved on their forehead, but it goes far deeper than that into the unseen.

The tapestry of God's Word has opened the infallible truth that humanity will be raped from the image of God to the image of the Beast. This is in migration and is being implemented through artificial intelligence, nano technology into fatal transhumanism. At this moment, almost eighty per cent of our daily devices and communications feature the rising form of artificial intelligence. This is the coming perfect storm that will ravage the planet as it peeks over the horizon through the eyes of the Beast. Every hour it is relentlessly consuming the masses. There are many others far better in educating this "lying wonder" and again I want to reinstate that my desire is not to study the license plate of the coming semi-truck, but to help us get out of its way.

Here is another momentary example of the techno-explosion opening a door that will not be shut. I want to preface that this is not indicting Elon Musk or his AI brain chip in a bad light. In many ways, technology has been a great service, but in the wrong hands, it can lead to the ultimate slavery. This week, I was far more shocked at the rising capstone of a "brain chip" to interface the computer and the internet into the psyche. Neural ink has implanted its first chip in a human brain.

The AI brain chip has been developed to be the size of a coin and is embedded in a person's skull. From the chip, an array of tiny wires, each roughly twenty times thinner than a human hair, fan out into the patient's brain. It was made to mesh the brain with artificial intelligence and computers. Its immediate future is to potentially revolutionize the way people with sensory or motor deficits might be able to interact and live more independently. The sobering question is could this lead to bring the image of the Beast to life. We witnessed the advent of television, the internet and then the computer open a 'Pandora's Box" leading to the unknown territory of the "Mark of the Beast."

The veiled dominance of global elitists will cancel any culture or individual that will not submit to this mark or its author. After the rescue of the remnant from the rapture, there will be a marriage of every demonic philosophy and the refining of the implosive "selfism." This will blanket the planet with a technical and spiritual unity that will eventually permeate every soul of men with another gospel under the False Prophet.

The Global Empire Begins Out of Order

Genesis 11

Now the whole world had one language and a common speech. As people moved eastward, they found a plain in Shinar and settled there. They said to each other, "Come, let's make bricks and bake them thoroughly." They used brick instead of stone, and tar for mortar. Then they said, "Come, let us build ourselves a city, with a tower that reaches to the heavens, so that we may make a name for ourselves; otherwise, we will be scattered over the face of the whole earth." But the LORD came down to see the city and the tower the people were building. The LORD said, "If as one people speaking the same language, they have begun to do this, then nothing they plan to do will be impossible for them. [7] Come, let us go down and confuse their language so they will not understand each other."

As with Israel, the brutal hand of the coming pharaoh is slowly tilting his boiling pot upon the nation, the church and your family to boil you a degree at a time. It is that simple and that true. In the Greek, the word for church was "ecclesia" meaning the "called out ones." From Abraham, God's people are called out of the present evil age to a place that He leads you. The world today is not a refuge, just another death camp. There is no neutral ground. In the Book of Matthew, Jesus said, "I will build my church", "my ecclesia." He was not talking about a building; He was talking about YOU. If you have been enlisted, are you serving, not being entangled in the affairs of civilian life. You must realize you have not only just been called; you must discover what you have been called out from.

The European Union rose, ironically, after the rebirth of Israel and began the convergence of the old Roman order. This new Roman international oligarchy began to realize the old Roman order. Paul Spaak was a former Belgian Prime Minister and one of the principal architects of what has since become the oracle of the European Union. He summed up the soul of the final global rebellion. His words were prophetic regarding the current meltdown into the global abyss. Spaak declared, "We do not want another committee, we have too many already. What we want is a man of sufficient stature to hold the allegiance of all people, and to lift us out of the economic morass into which we are sinking. Send us such a man, and be he god or devil, we will receive him."

This is a horrific statement at the heart of the devilish ploy for the New World Order. This quote takes some of the mystery away about why there is a tumultuous tsunami of evil in this present evil age? So, how has the sorcery overwhelmed society, how has it engulfed the nations, how has it tribalized the races, and how has it infiltrated all our families down to devastating the individual? We see the principle of lawlessness and sin saturating every crevice in societies. Dishonesty, promiscuous, murders, immorality and crime of every facet is plaguing all nations.

It is undeniable that the last eclipse of the tyranny of the world order is upon us in the consummation of the planned deception, so what do we hold on to?" The eclipse of humanity began with the lie in the garden of Eden and it will end in the gallows of the Antichrist. There is a saying that "if you tell the truth, it becomes part of your past. If you lie, it becomes part of your future." The "Great Lie" that we are the center, divorcing the truth is now the future we have sown.

This chapter puts me at risk for the peril of being accused of being a conspiracy theorist, Quite frankly, I hate having to speculate even from factual evidence, because it is not the point. This is why I have inserted scripture headlining every segment of this book.

A sad truth is since the assassinations of the Kennedys and Martin Luther King, the fact of the shadow government and the deep state are as plain as the nose on your face. Central Intelligence has become an oxymoron along with so many systems that have fallen. This is also why our focus cannot just be discerning the signs of the times, but the sign of Jonah.

I will try to minimize the remainder of this chapter because this is like having to testify against my father and my family. Please forgive my boldness, but we have not only lost our innocence, we have sold our soul as a nation as we are running out of time. I am not trying to be a prophet, but at this point, I truly declare that if there is not a reprieve this year from the veiled Marxist global regime, this will bring the "death of America" that radical Islam is boasting about. This great tragedy is even touted from our own universities.

The Deadly Puzzle Pieces of the Global Empire

Daniel 2

"You, O king, were watching; and behold, a great image! This great image, whose splendor was excellent stood before you; and its form was awesome. This image's head was of fine gold, its chest and arms of silver, its belly and thighs of bronze, its legs of iron, its feet partly of iron and partly of clay. You watched while a stone was cut out without hands, which struck the image on its feet of iron and clay, and broke them in pieces.

This is the large mural that hangs in the United Nations by Norwegian artist, Per Lasson Krohg, symbolizing the promise of "future global peace, liberty and security that dominates the east wall of the Security Council. It depicts a phoenix rising from its ashes to redeem the world from the Second World War. Above the dark sinister colors at the bottom are different images in bright colors symbolizing the hope for a better future. The upper center section shows a man and a woman both kneeling as flower children. The surrounding panels show people happy, singing and dancing while the lower section is dark and somber, showing a dungeon, dragon lairs, soldiers, and war machines. The people are struggling to free themselves from the bonds and chains. Krogh depicts a coiled dragon holding a sword in its mouth as it attempts to pull it out of its body. This is the wicked counterfeit Antichrist that rises out from this toxic spell.

Above the dragon, Krogh has painted a bridge and a sloping hill in which humans are climbing towards a brighter field above. These men, women and children are moving from each side of the sloping hill to meet in the middle where a white Phoenix stands with its wings unfolded, or is it truly a serpent with wings? The symbol of rising from the dark ashes to the light is inspired by the humanist agenda, not to achieve peace, and security, but to weave a worldwide web from sea to dimming sea.

The whole truth is that this mural represents the Marxist, Humanist "Gilded Lie" straight from Adam and Eve's fall from the rising serpent with wings in the garden of Eden. Under the Charter of the Security Council is said to be the primary responsibility for stewarding "international peace and security." The truth is it has been the birthing platform for the "New World Order" which is now being called the "Global Reset."

In the Book of First Thessalonians, and Revelation Six, the Apostle Paul and John warn us that this lawless spirit will bring the Antichrist to rise with his "Treaty with Death and Hell." This is the introduction the deceptive "White Horse of the Apocalypse" carrying a bow with no arrows that receives a global crown with deceptive false peace that will lead to destruction. This first seal of the Book of Revelation is the Antichrist riding into Jerusalem under the banner of "peace and safety." This employs the ten horned pedestal that the possessed global beast will stand.

The image of the U.N. in this mural has a phantom veneer conveying weakness in action from the past. It's probably safe to say that the average person's understanding of the U.N. boils down to the fact that it makes rules that the whole world is suggested to follow, and assists in global emergencies. This former quote, "we have ways to make you like it" is surfacing quickly. The fact is that this global beast is quickly growing teeth to devour national law to complete the new global Rome. Their suggestions are becoming commandments as the web of panic tightens through global war and plundering economics. These coalition of hybrid "men of renown are among us creating the web of slavery through technical delusion from Artificial Intelligence and the slanted media they possess. These enforcers are not kings from nations as once thought but a web of international beasts with financial and demonic mind control. If you look closer, you will understand who and where they are.

The Global Ten-Horned Beast

Revelation 17

The ten horns you saw are ten kings who have not yet received a kingdom, but who for one hour will receive authority as kings along with the beast. They have one purpose and will give their power and authority to the beast.

To understand this final global empire, we must continue to chase its roots. The ripple effects from Babylonian and Roman heritage in this time period cannot be overstated, especially Rome. The Roman Empire became the model for the coming last global empire. It is even located where the Caesar's once were seated. Its famous military, technology, and confiscated wealth gave it a glorious veneer but its moral depravity of sex temples and vomitorium were grave warnings of the fall that would eventually come from within.

Rome professed freedom and diversity Caesar and the elite, while the citizens were wrapped in taxes and domination. It claimed its power and military as the favor of the gods and even claimed the deity of its leaders as gods. Self-worship found its zenith in this empire and the perception of a true God was rendered absurd. They proclaimed democracy, yet three-fourths of the city of Rome were slaves. Rome was a regime of brute force and mercilessness. They crushed and consumed their neighbors with their iron fiber. Rome was the consummation of all of the fine culture consummated since the Days of Noah. All of Daniel's interpretations of world empires were connected through these mystical bestial kings.

The Greek word for Beast is "thereon" describing a wild animal that preys upon others. Carnal beasts have no spirit and thrive off of devouring what is in their path. But these Beasts of Revelation have a unified spirit that is derived from Satan to steal the planet from all humanity. The Antichrist will appear as a veiled, seductive personality in the physical realm. The location of the throne of the Antichrist and his False Prophet will certainly rise out of European Rome.

The seat of the Antichrist will sit upon a ten-horned pedestal of hybrid humans, not empires. It is clear that they are the presiding ten kings that are empowered ahead to rule from a borderless oligarchy among the global network. They are already weaving the web simultaneously to eventually give their control over to the Antichrist. The puppet strings attached to the first beast is an individual embodied in one particular man that will eventually mock the Messiah. He will then place his puppet strings to dominate and seduce these nationless ten kings to unite them in making the Beast the one sole arch regent of the final hour.

As the Antichrist rises to global power claiming "peace and security," he makes war with the remnant of Israel. He exercises his dominion over the nations and he removes three horns as he kills everyone who will not come under his full authority. He is the culmination of the previous four Beasts of Daniel. He comes out of the same tumultuous sea of nations that made the previous empire. This Beast is worshipped as god, like the former Caesars and kings. This "Man of Sin" will be seductive, charismatic and exceedingly attractive on the surface, but he is the incarnation from hell.

This Beast is unique from the others; whereas they are consenting human hybrids, groomed and apparent, he is the angelic hybrid king of Satan falsely resurrecting in the rebuilt temple where he assumes complete authority. I am convinced that these ten kings with no kingdom are among us today being groomed by evil spirits to infuse the preparation for the Antichrist. Their weapons of warfare are derivatives of artificial intelligence, technology, power, and garnered wealth to divest the masses of control. This will conclude with the Mark of the Beast in the global technocracy.

Nothing can match the dark history that corresponds to this ethereal confederacy subdued by their hybrid king. This evil conspiracy will ascend by controlling all of humanity through the Mark of the Beast and will destroy anyone that does not submit to their will. The Antichrist then begins to even turn on his own. The ten kings are reduced and sifted to seven as three, and he devours the mystery Harlot because she has served her purpose. The remaining sifted rebels will bow to the Antichrist and his False Prophet, and will share in their destruction. This reigning Beast has the name "blasphemy" because he claims to be God.

The Mysterious Harlot as the Puzzling Piece

Then the angel carried me away in the Spirit into a wilderness. There I saw a woman sitting on a scarlet beast that was covered with blasphemous names and had seven heads and ten horns. The woman was dressed in purple and scarlet, and was glittering with gold, precious stones and pearls. She held a golden cup in her hand, filled with abominable things and the filth of her adulteries. When I saw her, I was greatly astonished. Then the angel said to me: "Why are you astonished? I will explain to you the mystery of the woman and of the beast she rides, which has the seven heads and ten horns.

Two years ago, I witnessed a terrifying video on the internet on an Olympic celebration in the heart of Europe. It was a complete revelation of the final apocalyptic kingdom from the days of the prophet Daniel in motion. It was a complete exposure of the final global assault of politics, and spiritual deception in the midst of the concluding empire of the rising Beast in relationship with the mysterious Harlot of Babylon being in the midst. To put this in context, a few weeks before this, I was inspired to create the art piece above of the theme of the final New World Order and its global participants for a new writing. It is a vision of the Mysterious Harlot with her cup, riding the Beast of Revelation, represented by the Bestial false god of Molech. Behind them is the fiery Tower of Babel as the backdrop. It is the cover of my future book, "The Harlot's Cup at the Twilights Last Gleaming." A few days later is when I witnessed an astonishing video filmed at the opening of the Commonwealth Olympic Games located in Birmingham, England. It was seen by a third of the world and comprised seventy-two nations that will be the home base for the Antichrist. The opening photos below just gives a glimpse into the satanic occultic ritual that opened the Olympics. It contained every article that is revealed on the book cover, yet it went even further, as there were surrounding witches with occultic glowing crystals worshipping the Beast with its glowing eyes in the arena from hell.

Little did I realize how arrogant the Prince of this World has become and how the inhabitants of the earth have been so intoxicated by the Mystery of Lawlessness coming from the Harlot's cup. It deeply convicted me on how urgent the trumpet must be blown regardless of who is offended nationally, individually or spiritually.

This is the vision the Apostle John gave in the Book of Revelation. As John was carried away by the Holy Spirit, he was absolutely astonished at the horrific site than he saw upon the earth. John was witnessing a betrayal even greater than Judas taking place in the final hour. He saw this faithless woman that had betrayed her Creator and how she sat on the Beast forsaking everything that she was created for. She was drunk on the blood of those that were bearing witness to the One she had betrayed. From this point, we will peer into the most devastating mystery in the history of histories.

One of the greatest debates concerning Biblical eschatology is Mystery Babylon, the Harlot and her partnering Beast. This mysterious Harlot is without a doubt the producing architect of a cauldron of sorcery in the last day. As Israel followed Jezebel, all the nations are now following her as they once followed the previous wicked queen from the first corporate witness. This woman has earned the title of "the great whore" because she sold herself for comfort and luxury. She sits on her throne and proclaims that she will never taste the suffering that others have ingested. She is separated and protected by the waters of the planet as the other nations traffic with her. But even the oceans cannot protect her from the coming fire.

The word "whore" comes from the Greek word "porne," which is translated "pornography" and "fornicator." At this point, she has fallen from being the greatest witness and exporter of the Gospel to the greatest exporter of pornography. To commit fornication is to commit any sexual act for wealth. Throughout the Bible, in a spiritual sense, a fornicator would refer to anyone who worships or serves other "gods" rather than the one true God and Creator as Lord. This Harlot has an arrogant spirit that has deceived her into thinking she still holds her former glory. She once was a cup in the hand of the Lord, but now she feeds her cup to the nations full of sorcery. She has become spiritually inverted and she thrives on her sensuality and material wealth.

This Harlot has truly spawned the last stage of a global false religion, departed from the one true God. She consents to all religion of polytheism, pantheism, hedonism, and assembles the harem of modern religions gain from the former empires, into a global deception that will usher in the worship of the Antichrist. The whore of Babylon is spiritually adulterous with the Beast and the kings of the earth mixing her potion with empirical and moral decadence. Her sorcery of fornication has ended up in the locality of the where it originated.

A final strand of the rising unified global religion has recently come under the auspice and wings of the Roman Pope, and a core of godless interfaith children gathered at Mount Sinai. They have joined in unity to erase the Ten Commandments with new ones under the name of "climate change." This grievous rebellion began an interfaith initiative connected to the United Nations to force the global government to accept the "New Ten Commandments."

Their opening Sunday service began with an Israeli environmental activist smashing a set of mocking tablets of the Ten Commandments on the peak of Mount Sinai, symbolizing the failure of the order of the nations to protect "Mother Earth." It is centered on the blasphemous mandate of "climate repentance." These so-called ten commandments are based upon the twisted principles that creation manifests "divinity." They also command to change our "inner climate" and repent from not worshipping "Gaia, the mother earth." This declares the same warning from the Lord Jesus to the apostate Pharisees in the "Seven Woes" as He exposed them with, "you always resist the Holy Spirit." The greatest sin is the ascending demonic spirits they have not resisted.

There are no prostitutes or harlots that are born that way. They are developed through temptation and time, sometimes centuries. There is always a past of innocence that morphs into a woman selling herself. There is no beast that is born that way either. It is about the growth of pride into violence and rage from never learning the truth. These two most dramatic figures rise in self-glory in the Tribulation which are the adulterous Harlot that is riding upon a brutal Beast that spans the globe. She has betrayed her faithful Eternal Husband and is having an affair with this carnal Beast that will quickly turn and devour her. She is so corrupt and evil that God refuses to touch her so her demise is given over to the Beast. No one wants to discover their mother they learned to love is a harlot. More times than not, we end up leaving it at the door of denial or blaming God. This has to stop because it only retards our healing.

Escaping the Collapsing Global Web

Revelation 11

I was given a reed like a measuring rod and was told, "Go and measure the temple of God and the altar, with its worshipers. But exclude the outer court; do not measure it, because it has been given to the Gentiles. They will trample on the holy city for 42 months. And I will appoint my two witnesses, and they will prophesy 1,260 days, clothed in sackcloth." They are "the two olive trees" and the two lampstands, and "they stand before the Lord of the earth.

We need to understand the fatal destruction of the first Babylon as it fell under the son of Nebuchadnezzar as he took the stolen vessels of the temple to indulge in an orgy. The ax was finally laid to the roots as the mysterious hand of God appeared writing on the banquet hall, "Mene, Mene Tekel, meaning you have been weighed and been found wanting, The Lord numbered their night for not repenting of committing blasphemy. Is that very Hand of God about to write on the wall of our banquet hall in the nominal church? Do we return from the adultery of the banquet hall and theater or do we continue selling a message that has left the remnant wanting more.

I am so grieved how Israel has continued to fall into the web of self-determination and Messianic confusion. There has never been more fervor in Israel over rebuilding the Temple and are even looking at destroying the Dome of the Rock that sets on the Temple Mount. This would induce a word war beyond description. This sets the trap for the Antichrist to come with this olive branch to set a condensed Temple beside the third most revered Islamic Dome of the Rock. Sovereignly, this is not a fatal flaw but a final exodus into the Valley of Decision.

I am also so grieved how are nation has fallen into the web of "selfism" leaving Generation Y and Z drowning from a lack of vision and hope. They have been taught the irony and myth that the Bible is outdated and irrelevant. They have been schooled to trust in the maddening web of perceptive media that is flowing from the heart of the global lie that it is "all about me." Our history is being rewritten before their eyes to extract any eternal preeminence or image of God. Yet, there is a faint "glistening of Light" of revival among this generation and our mission must be to reach these hurting brilliant kids.

Yet, my greatest agony is the apathetic nominal church and our nation's betrayal of our God, just as Israel has done. We have also betrayed our children because our temples have become full of the idols of apathy and theater that they are not buying, because they see through it. If we do not come out and be separate, we will certainly be left behind to face the Day of Evil.

Here are the lyrics to a song of mine from several years ago.

The Web
The day of destruction is drawing so near
His voice of deception has stirred all you fear
A thread from the power
A thread from the gold
A thread of desire that's driven your soul
Into the web of the reaper
Into the dark of the night
Is his web of delusion
He will squeeze out your life
Come into the net of salvation

CHAPTER NINE

The Sifting of Our Nation at Ground Zero?

Revelation 18

"'Fallen! Fallen is Babylon the Great!'

She has become a dwelling for demons

and a haunt for every impure spirit,

a haunt for every unclean bird,

a haunt for every unclean and detestable animal.

For all the nations have drunk

the maddening wine of her adulteries.

The kings of the earth committed adultery with her,

and the merchants of the earth grew rich from her excessive luxuries."

"If a man has no purpose, his life is just a continuous death?"
Pierre Bolste

God slowly revealed to me where the current of this age is taking us as I faced three decades in the godless whirlwind of Colorado's juvenile justice system. It was a paradox of having the experience of great joy and great agony by the sifting of thousands of shattered hearts in incarcerated kids. In spite of the godless charade of the system, there were many who surrendered their lives to Jesus Christ, and there were many more that rejected Him as Savior. It was devastating watching the anchor of the faithful grandma in the black community fade away and watch the lethal trap of gang life and drugs swallow up an entire abandoned generation. In unison, it has been just as difficult watching the nuclear faith in our community and culture being eclipsed by social media and fractured families. Here is an example of what life in the trenches of young people are about.

I suffered a great tragedy several years ago when my nephew, Doug died from his fatal bout with Leukemia. I was scheduled to do a service at a youth detention facility, but it was the last thing that I felt like doing. Regardless, I deeply understood the necessity to continue. When I got there, we began with music and I then started the message that I had prepared for. At this point, I looked over and there was a young man with a face of rage as he looked at me with pure hatred. I tried to ignore it, but it continued to get worse. Then the Lord took over and things got extremely intense.

I bizarrely turned and began to speak about an incident where I contracted an abscessed tooth that caused my jaw to swell in intense pain. I had to do something because the pain was unbearable. As I got in to see the dentist, he pulled out a scalpel that quenched the tremendous pain. As he lanced my gum, it was a mess, but I almost passed out from the relief. I wondered where this rabbit trail was leading to.

I then turned around in the meeting and looked straight into the eyes of this young man writhing in pain that was disguised in rage. I then said, "Someone in this meeting is experiencing a similar pain, but it is his soul that needs to be lanced. This triggered one of the most intense experiences in my ministry. He put his head in his lap and began to howl like a wolf over and over. The kids in the meeting looked with terror and confusion as he continued in pain. I knew that I had to do something, so I picked him up to carry him out of the room as I asked the volunteers to continue the music.

As I got Jeff into the next room, I just held him as he wept bitterly. His life had finally come to a head as his fear erupted. I spoke to him through the passion of Christ. I said, "I know you want God's help but you're afraid He'll abandon you too?"

The second was, "This is about your parents, isn't it?" He continues sobbing as he shook his head in agreement. After he was able to talk, Jeff told me that his mother had abandoned him at two years old and his dad had just disappeared on him, leaving him alone in the system. I then asked Jeff if he was ready to let God into his life.

He began to weep even deeper as he shook his head in agreement. I then told him that I knew it was the fear of being abandoned again and I assured him that this would heal the abandonment in his life. That was the day that the healing began in Jeff's life and He was never the same.

The Final Invasion of the Great Lie

2 Thessalonians 2

*The coming of the lawless one will be in accordance with how Satan works. He will use all sorts of displays of power through signs and wonders that serve the lie, and all the ways that wickedness deceives those who are perishing. They perish because they refused to love the truth and so be saved. For this reason, God sends them a powerful delusion so that they **will believe the lie** and so that all will be condemned who have not believed the truth but have delighted in wickedness.*

Jesus warned that the ravages of war would be a critical birth pain that would turn the page of time. As a very young man, my dad and his family of eighteen were sitting in front of the radio when the special bulletin pronounced the bombing of Pearl Harbor. The next day, he was in the recruiting office on his way to the beaches of Normandy. He knew he really had no choice. They were defined as the "greatest generation" as participants in sacrifices of the highest order. His suffering sacrifice defined the rest of his life and has continued to be my greatest lesson from him. The fatigue from the world wars set in as all of the dads returned home to hide from exhaustion. They just wanted their lives back.

It is devastating witnessing the paradigm shift from our nation's courage of conviction to completely losing our innocence. Young people today are trapped in a carnival of pleasure and pain, longing for acceptance and a reason for existence. Not that long ago, I had a large group of incarcerated boys, I asked them the direct question, "If we were attacked as a nation would you answer the call to go to war? In shock, not one kid would even consider it. There were two responses. The first answer was, "What in this country is worth fighting for?" and the second was, "What would that do for me?" This tragically revealed they were reduced to self-survival and no eternal understanding of life. The truth to this is almost too hard to bear.

Since time that the Bible has labeled irrelevant and outdated by the secular circus that we are drowning in, our kids are drowning without it. The returned spiritual lawlessness and corruption from the Days of Noah is being redefined with a new implosive gospel with a new age roadmap.

The Sabotage of Generational Harlotry

Romans 8

For although they knew God, they neither glorified him as God nor gave thanks to him, but their thinking became futile and their foolish hearts were darkened. Although they claimed to be wise, they became fools and exchanged the glory of the immortal God for images made to look like a mortal human being and birds and animals and reptiles.

"Bad company is as instructive as licentiousness. One makes up for the loss of one's innocence with the loss of one's prejudices." Denis Diderot

America the Beautiful lost its innocence when we stopped looking up from our knees. The tremendous upheaval in living standards, in attitudes toward faith, and in moral foundations cratered in the name of the trinity of me, myself and I. The most lethal foundation of our corporate fall was the basis of amoralism. I had a great fall as a young man morally, but I knew it was wrong. To be amoral is the delusion that you just do not realize what you're doing is wrong. The author Robert Louis Stevenson, coined the word amoral to differentiate from being immoral. The greatest danger of being amoral is an empty cycle of lawless existence with no boundaries rather than being judgmentally sound.

This is now a generational curse being passed from one generation to the next. Some perceive it as tolerance for new ways, equality of rights, removing many prejudices of sexual, racial and moral origin. It has defined as the freedom to live on individual preference with no accountability to anyone, especially God and the Bible.

Here is a summary of the generations from the Civil War.

- **The Lost Generation (1883-1900)**

  This was the generation spinning after the Civil War through World War One into the Industrial Revolution. The Lost Generation grew up in the paradigm shift from the farm to the city. They were the first consumers. and media-saturated.

- **The Greatest Generation (1901-1924)**

  This generation came after the insufferable "Roaring Twenties," and the Great Depression to be the participants in the sacrifice of the highest order through World War Two.

- **The Silent Generation (1925-1945)**

  This generation started as fathers came home to their families in deep pain from the war effort. They were characterized as traditionalists as technology from the war began to consume them.

- **The Baby Boomers (1946-1964)**

  The wheels came off in this generation during a personal and cultural implosion where lawlessness turned the love of most to grow cold toward God and one another.

- **Generation X (1965-1980)**

  As the children of the seventies and the eighties, this group shifted societal values as they were called the "latchkey generation" returning from school to an empty home.

- **Gen Y / Millennials (1981-1996)**

  This was the first generation to grow up with the internet. Millennials have also been described as the first global generation. It is no marvel because it is named the "worldwide web."

- **Generation Z (1997-2010)**

  From the violation of trust, they have turned to drowning in the cistern of relativism. They brilliantly pursue the desert of unbelief in agony. Relativism has taught this nothing is set in stone, just quicksand.

The Great Lie Blossoming in the Sorcerous Sixties

For there are many, of whom I have often told you, and now tell you even with tears, who live as enemies of the cross of Christ whose fate is destruction, whose god is their worldly appetite, their sensuality, and whose glory is in their shame, who focus their mind on earthly and temporal things.

Born approximately 1950 – 1972 (Late Boomers and Generation X)

The innocence of the nation was raped in the advent of the Sixties. Many of the core values of this turbulent period remain alive in malignant ways in present day America. Some Christians dismiss the Sixties as just a period of exploration. Others, however understood the decadence exposing the decade for many of the ills that trouble contemporary America. Rome's belly-buttoned meaning of life found its final home in our wandering heart of apathy and indulgence. It birthed a rampant global anesthetic with no regard for the eternal answer to an eternal future.

Growing up in the "eye of the storm" at the end of the "Sixties" gave me a bird's eye view watching the spiritual storm collapsing the nation into apostasy. It became a collage of personal and cultural implosions, most that turned the love of most to grow cold toward God and one another. Concurrently, with the unmatched journey to the moon, the lancing of tribal racial tensions, the challenge of seductive politics and apostate religion, it seeded the final rebellion and the numbness that would eventually deeply mark the age. As we forgot the Lord, the master of deception came through the back door kidnapping our kids.

The New Age crystalized the public consciousness through the corrosive "selfism," attending to crystals, reincarnation, and the channeling of "ascended masters" as I wondered where are they ascending from? We didn't even ask. They were beginning their rise from the "abyss" from Genesis as it is re-rooted the worship of "mother earth." For some, it was defined as the dawning of a spiritual New Age and to others a grasp for power through the complicit New World Order. The truth is it was introducing the marriage of the Harlot and the Beast.

As we traveled this grazing maze treading the spiritual waters of rebellion, we began to visit our sins upon the next generation to the next. The contaminating brew from the cup of the Harlot of Babylon began to intoxicate the nations. The Prince of this World taught us the "gospel of toxic pride" that makes you the center of the universe with the new age mantra to "create your own reality." As it taught the world revolves around you, it spun a web covering the globe casting its spell of harlotry.

Understanding Generation Why?

2 Thessalonians 1

All this is evidence that God's judgment is right, and as a result you will be counted worthy of the kingdom of God, for which you are suffering. God is just: He will pay back trouble to those who trouble you and give relief to you who are troubled, and to us as well. This will happen when the Lord Jesus is revealed from heaven in blazing fire with his powerful angels. He will punish those who do not know God and do not obey the gospel of our Lord Jesus. They will be punished with everlasting destruction and shut out from the presence of the Lord and from the glory of his might on the day he comes to be glorified in his holy people and to be marveled at among all those who have believed. This includes you, because you believed our testimony to you.

Born approximately 1981 – 1996

From the Bible, "My City, My God' by the International Bible Society

Above is the cover of a Bible released by the International Bible Society that has the story of one of my incarcerated kids. He had been hiding in services for years without me knowing it.

One Sunday morning when I was doing church in a juvenile detention center in Colorado, a young man stood up in the second row and threw his chair at me. I just smiled with concern and responded, "Well, at least I guess I got your attention." The staff rushed over and removed him to isolation as I realized how desperate he was.

When I came back on Monday night for Bible study, Rusty was sitting there waiting for me with his arms crossed, with a face of rage. The more I went through the study, the angrier he became. All of a sudden, one of the guys looked at him and said, "Whoa, dude, you look like a vampire!" I responded with, "Son, we don't talk to each other like that," but I have to admit when I looked back at him, I saw it too as I wondered where this was going.

I proceeded to the end of our meeting and Rusty came up and said, "I have to talk to you right now!!" I told him that I would get the other guys back and then come to get him. We sat down together and his first words were "You hurt me!!" I responded with, "Son, I don't know you and I've never touched you. How did I hurt you?" He put his hand over his heart his and just glared at me. He then told me he had been seeing me preaching at the different facilities he had been in. He told me that this had happened every time.

It then began to add up that this was the conviction in his heart and soul. We continued to talk and Rusty gave me an intense look and said, "You make no sense to me!! I can tell you love me but you don't know me!" He later explained his frustration that if I really knew him, I couldn't love him. He also told me that no one can love somebody they don't know. I then told Rusty that God can. The Lord put it on my heart to tell him that if he didn't get the severity of coming to Christ, he wouldn't make it six more months.

With tears in his eyes, Rusty got up and told me he wanted to go back to his room. When I came back to do church the next week, Rusty was waiting for me with a glowing, peaceful face that was nothing like his encounter before. He shared with me, "I did it. I gave my life to Jesus." We sat down and Rusty explained to me his history that at six years old, his father left him for dead and that he hated men. He then shared how he had gone from Satanism into a vampire cult getting addicted to drinking blood in a desperate search for some kind of power and control in his life. Rusty had the sins of his father visit him with a life of rage and desperation, but God's graceful hand reached down and pulled him from the fire.

After he was released, we went to do the photo shoot in Five Points for the story in the Bible, Rusty pointed to something in this parking lot and he asked me, "Do you see that?" I said that I didn't see anything and he asked me again and then said, "Don't you see that dumpster?" when I said, "Sure." He then told me that it was his house for years. Rusty led his vampire cult where they cruised doing the unspeakable.

This even continued the next year when the Bible was released. I was giving them out at a girl's facility when this little girl came up with a horrible look on her face and screamed, "Who is this?!" I said that is Rusty, a boy that gave his life to God. She gasped and said, "No way! I used to drink blood with him! He would never do that. He was the most wicked person that I've ever known!" Amazingly, that night in church she and her friend also gave their life to God. This chain of lost souls came from the devastation of abusive fathers. Rusty could have been the poster boy for the coming prodigal generations.

Generation Y, which are mostly named "Millennials," have followed Generation X into the jungle of maddening apostasy. They grew up as orphans as digital natives who saw the transition to technology as an umbilical cord to post-Christian America. Generation Y grew up as a digital native who has seen the transition of bathing in technology and adapting to every breath. With various unique characteristics and values, Millennials have wandered the desert of unbelief in a godless society like a "dog without a bone."

Technology caused the rapid de-evolution of how people communicated and relational issues continued to decline. As Baby Boomers grew up with television expanding a mythic perception, techno madness exploded even further as the computer revolution was taking hold, and Millennials came of age during the internet explosion. Across the globe, Millennials have postponed marriage or living together as a couple. Their moral compass continued to spin from not having a true spiritual foundation. This black hole has continued as we now witness the last letter Z, bring us to the point of no return.

The Final Plight of Generation Z

2 Timothy 3

But mark this: There will be terrible times in the last days. People will be lovers of themselves, lovers of money, boastful, proud, abusive, disobedient to their parents, ungrateful, unholy, without love, unforgiving, slanderous, without self-control, brutal, not lovers of the good, treacherous, rash, conceited, lovers of pleasure rather than lovers of God, having a form of godliness but denying its power.

Born approximately 1997 – 2015

Normal is not coming back, Jesus is. Anonymous

There is a story of a young man in the mountains of Colorado that neglectfully fell off a cliff as he grabbed a protruding branch, keeping him from careening down hundreds of feet. In panic, he screamed out, "Is anybody there?!" Suddenly, the clouds parted as a calm Voice spoke, "Son, let go and I'll catch you." He replied, "this is all I have, I can't let go!" The Voice spoke again to let go. The young man still twisting in the wind finally screams out again, "Is there anybody else up there?!"

This final generation is grasping for straws because they have been starved into death. The last generation of Generation Z has reached the pinnacle of "selfism" and self-determination, leaving nowhere else to go but up. The spiritual and moral landslide

138

has continued, burying them alive under the spell of unbelief. They are also defined as the "zoomers" for very good reasons. They are hurling forward off the cliff with no vision, as they are reaching for the stars.

This is a sobering "selfie" of Generation Z. Only one in ten young people in Generation Z trust the established media, thank God. Less than one in five say that they can trust public education or the government, thank God again. In their skepticism, they have embraced the internet and social media to critique institutions easily and see through double standards, having no idea they have been swallowed whole by a more ferocious beast. From the violation of trust, they have turned to drowning in the cistern of relativism. Relativism has taught this generation that nothing is set in stone, just quicksand.

This generation now stand at the edge of the cliff of the last stage of rebellion. They are at the door of the coming tribulation without a clue as their father's sins and forgetfulness have caused their blindness. These are not the seeds that they have sown. The indulging pagan philosophies of Rome and Greece have been branded on them without even knowing it. Moral relativism has come to fruition in Gen Z, and has blossomed into a huge global tree with the foul birds of the air in its branches shadowing the entire planet. What is morally right and wrong has morphed into the lawlessness in society from the gospel of rancid media.

This has actually been a ferocious battle since the inception of the nation in 1776. From the beginning, our nation had a great debate between patriot believers and theists over "the pursuit of happiness" or "the pursuit of holiness." At this point, we now see this lawlessness has completely overshadowed this generation. Our government, our educational system, the media, the fermenting philosophies, and our technology have paved the broad road from Rome leading to destruction. We have not only not learned from history; we are repeating it with an addiction for more.

I used to think that nothing comes after the letter "Z," but I was wrong. Here is a tragic description of what they call, a blossoming "Generation Alpha. It is the most materially endowed generation ever, the most technologically savvy generation entering the black hole of unbelief. While they are the youngest generation, they have inherited the same brand or mark of ownership. They are already mastering social media as culture consumers being consumed. The brutal truth is what is coming after Gen Z will be Jesus Christ, the Messiah from the heavens. My prayer is this generation will reach out from the rope that is about to hang them to grasp the hand of their Redeemer.

The Final Dawn of Deception

1 Thessalonians 5

Now, brothers and sisters, about times and dates we do not need to write to you, for you know very well that the day of the Lord will come like a thief in the night. While people are saying, "Peace and safety," destruction will come on them suddenly, as labor pains on a pregnant woman, and they will not escape. But you, brothers and sisters, are not in darkness so that this day should surprise you like a thief. You are all children of the light and children of the day. We do not belong to the night or to the darkness. So then, let us not be like others, who are asleep, but let us be awake and sober. For those who sleep, sleep at night, and those who get drunk, get drunk at night.

In 1983, the British author William Golding, wrote a novel called "The Lord of the Flies." The theme of the novel is an attempt to trace the defects of society to the defects of human nature. There are children evacuated because of a nuclear war, left in the ruins of a failed culture. After a plane crash, these kids have to fashion their own society. Their attempts at establishing a social order gradually devolves into savagery. Finally abandoning all moral constraints, the boys commit murder before they are rescued. The moral is that the shape of a society must depend on the ethical nature of the individual and not on any political system however apparently logical or respectable." It must be understood that the roots of ethics can only sprout from a Biblical mandate through His Spirit.

This is a parable of the global village being led by vicious, blood thirsty leaders in the extended adolescence of the empires stemming from the Tower of Babel. The mile markers closely behind us and all the signs before us all point to the new Babel and the final city of Rome with the Harlot providing her cup of intoxicants. Since 1987, there have been false believers of an esoteric prophecy of the need for the earth's "counterfeit cleansing" that is consummating under the banner of "climate change." This has married the contrived "new age harmonic convergence" that touts "peace and security" that the Antichrist enters the gates of the Tribulation with. According to these preceding devilish prophets, this convergence will end the hellish earth pains, beginning the new age of universal peace. The emerging global society will no longer be shackled by the truth and a Lord, as they choose their own destruction.

As humanity continues reaching for the stars to validate godhood, as in Babel and Rome, they once again turn to worship the earth through the black hole of "selfism." The Age of Reason concluded the genesis in the way where man viewed himself, the pursuit of knowledge, and the universe from a godless delusion. It returned mankind to assuming he was the reason for his brightness that he inherited from Lucifer. Reason, rationality and self-enlightenment returned and was touted as the "new gods" from its Roman and Babylonian roots.

The so-called "World Wide Web" is now evangelized through technology and social media. There will soon be an intentional apocalyptic collapse to reorder its intent. We must finally realize the "Lizard of Oz" is already pulling the levers behind the curtain, before he sits as the dark prince on the throne of the seething world order. This throne is deceptively adorned with the royalty of the first tyrant Nimrod. From the beginning, humanity has fallen gullibly to foolish "men of renown" because we look for idols, we can put our hands on. We truly must find our knees because many leaders standing behind the podium no longer having the answer. In fact, they don't even understand the questions anymore.

I remember well when the first globalist president Barah Obama spoke in his last term to warn our nation that "the rest of the world is not going to allow us to live the way we do." As the global shift is sifting even further in our nation politically, economically, and spiritually, we have fallen asleep at the wheel. It doesn't matter what the world thinks, the real issue is whether the Lord is going to allow you to live the way we do.

THE SIFTING HARVEST
THROUGH THE TRIBULATION

CHAPTER TEN

The Coming Hour of Trial for Planet Earth

Revelation 14

Then I looked, and behold, a white cloud, and on the cloud sat *One* like the Son of Man, having on His head a golden crown, and in His hand a sharp sickle. And another angel came out of the temple, crying with a loud voice to Him who sat on the cloud, "Thrust in Your sickle and reap, for the time has come for You to reap, for the harvest of the earth is ripe."

"My views are changing as the world itself is changing. The truth is my main view." Tucker Carlsen

Many years ago, my youngest son and I went rafting in summer in the Colorado mountains at the height of the runoff of the Colorado river. Before we entered the raft, the guide warned us that because of the intense rapids someone might fall out. He then said, "If this happens, grab them by the top of their life preserver and shove them under the water to get them back in the raft." My son then looked at me in horror, and said, "Dad, can we go home?"

A critical exhortation from the Apostle Paul to Timothy and for us all at this time is "For God did not give us a spirit of timidity or cowardice or fear, but He has given us a spirit of power and of love and of sound judgment and personal discipline. I am sure if you have read this far, you do not need to fear the judgement of this world, because you have passed over. In fact, if we truly reverentially fear God, you have nothing left to fear. Christ disciplines those He loves, but He never leaves them in despair.

The lens of my life magnified in my young age of rebellion after being abandoned by my father. Christ stopped me at the edge of the cliff and pushed me under the waters as I faced decades in prison as He saved me from myself. It broke me as He baptized me with the comforting words, "Son, it's over." In the following month, the Lord did an unspeakable deliverance that became the axis for my life. I got to come home.

From that moment, my life has actually not gotten any easier, just more awesome. I have learned slowly the meaning, "You shall know the truth and the truth will set you free." Through fire, I now understand that facing the truth can be daunting and fearful as it produces eternal fruit. Day by day, my heart and soul are still getting it, but if you will surrender and let the Holy Spirit be your compass. It will bring you to life with vision to be a chosen witness.

Proverbs Twenty-One warns us that "a false witness will perish, but a careful listener will testify successfully." It seems obscure that witnessing is truly about listening. The Book of Revelation tells every church and overcomer, "Whoever has ears, let them hear what the Spirit says to the churches." The word "witness" appears in God's Word more than one hundred times. A witness is one who sees an event and testifies to it. This implies two things. First that a witness has personal experience of the event, and next, because of this personal experience, this witness has been martyred by the knowledge of the truth.

I apologize somewhat, but not really, that I have tried to keep this from being another rehash, and readdressing what others have already written about the signs of our times. Once again, the priority of this book is to help prepare the remnant with the priority of God's Word in the moment. I have yearned to stay within the shattered veil of the Messiah's heart over the raging current of this present evil age from the passion of conviction.

Being a witness can be uncomfortable and brutal, especially today. Resistance to the conviction of the Holy Spirit has extinguished nominal church. The saying, "the truth hurts" is valid. Truth today is simply on the "endangered species list." The whole truth and nothing but the truth, so help me God, is no longer a vow, but it can get you charged with a hate crime.

We must honestly ask ourselves, "Is there enough evidence to convict you of truly following the Lord Jesus?" Paul said to "examine yourselves to see whether you are in the faith; test yourselves." It is our responsibility to have a sense of urgency as we realize we are staring eternity in the face.

The Coming Sifting Blade of the Messiah

Matthew 24

"Therefore, when you see the 'abomination of desolation,' spoken of by Daniel the prophet, standing in the holy place" (whoever reads, let him understand), "then let those who are in Judea flee to the mountains. Let him who is on the housetop not go down to take anything out of his house. And let him who is in the field not go back to get his clothes. But woe to those who are pregnant and to those who are nursing babies in those days! And pray that your flight may not be in winter or on the Sabbath. For then there will be great tribulation, such as has not been since the beginning of the world until this time, no, nor ever shall be. And unless those days were shortened, no flesh would be saved; but for the elect's sake those days will be shortened.

Years ago, Senator Barry Goldwater was running for the presidency of the nation when he did the unthinkable as he detoured from "political correctness." At that time, nuclear war was a major phobia, far worse than he must have realized. He brashly spoke up concerning the jungle warfare in Viet Nam and said, "We need to knock the leaves off the trees with a nuclear bomb to see who we are fighting. He was radically addressing the century of jungle warfare the enemy had fought that made our technology worthless. It was obviously a metaphor, but it cost him the election.

Sometimes, the truth hurts. In concern that what I am saying will be taken completely out of context, the truth at this point is not an option. As the planet shakes from residual spiritual anarchy and lawlessness, something is about to give. I am getting this out of the way so we can end with the true heart of God's desires. I assure you the Messiah is about to shake the leaves off the trees and expose the nakedness of the global masses in rebellion that is the true enemy.

The sifting blade of the Messiah has already begun the imminent global sifting of His faithful remnant as He will descend as a "thief in the night" to rob the earth of the "restrainer." This current restrainer is the one who is holding back and hindering the advance of the Antichrist, preventing the satanic kingdom from destroying the planet before the tribulation opens.

The final judgement will not come until the Antichrist rides into Jerusalem on the counterfeit white horse of the apocalypse. He enters proclaiming "peace and security" for Israel and the globe. Since their return from the Diaspora, Israel has been at war continually with the survival mode in one hand as the other hand is flirting with the romance of all things secular. Except for a remnant, they continue to reject their Messiah King, and they will soon be captivated under a king from this world promising "peace and security" as the "troubles of Jacob" conclude.

The dispensation of the Church Age is the period of time from Pentecost to the closing rapture. It is called the Church Age because it covers the period in which the Church was to function on earth as the mediator. It was to correspond as the dispensation of Grace. This debacle will be covered later. This chapter will be condensed because it defines the coming eclipse after the faithful remnant have shut the door of the church age on their way out. It is more about the sifting judgement from the entering Tribulation of the world and the coming sifting fire.

As the age of grace closes, the Tribulation commences as the blade of sifting will begin to cleanse the earth with fire, as the Israelites receive their former mantle from the Old Covenant to complete the mission of the Gospel. The remnant of Israel will pick up where the faithful church left off. There will be 144,000 Jews that are "sealed," with a special protection of God. They are kept safe from the divine judgments and from the wrath of the Antichrist.

Their mission is to evangelize the post-rapture world and proclaim the gospel during the tribulation period. The 144,000 are an amazing intervention, but they are "removed" through the fire of martyrdom. As a result of their mission, "a great multitude that no one could count, from every nation, tribe, people and language" will come to faith in Christ.

The final gate of salvation closes at the end of the Great Tribulation as two witnesses appear to complete the mission from the Old Covenant. Moses and Elijah are the two witnesses in the Great Tribulation that confront the Antichrist. These two returning witnesses will have the power to turn water into blood, which duplicates a prior miracle of Moses. And the witnesses will have the power to destroy their enemies with fire , which corresponds to an event in Elijah's life. At the end of their ministry, the Antichrist kills them as the wicked world will rejoice, allowing the bodies of the fallen prophets to lie in the streets. Then the Messiah's blade will be laid to the roots.

The World's Ripened Harvest in the Tribulation

Joel 3

For there I will sit to judge all the surrounding nations.

Put in the sickle, for the harvest is ripe.

Come, go down;

For the winepress is full,

The vats overflow,

For their wickedness is great."

Multitudes, multitudes in the valley of decision!

For the Day of the LORD is near in the valley of decision.

"Oh, what a tangled web we weave, when first we practice to deceive!"
Sir Walter Scott

The phrase the "Day of the Lord" identifies the events that take place at the end of human history. It identifies the span of time during which God personally intrudes again, to directly fulfil His concluding sifting plan for humanity. The Day of the Lord will be a longer period of time than just a single day. Its climax is when Christ will return and cleanses heaven and earth in preparation for the eternal state of all mankind in the Valley of Decision.

The New Testament calls this period both "the Day of Wrath," and the complimenting "Day of Visitation." This comprises the bewildering and glorious fulfillment when God's wrath wills be poured out on the unbelieving world after the remnant of the church has been sifted above. Besides being a time of judgment, it will also be a time of great salvation as God will deliver the remnant of Israel, forgiving their sins and restoring His chosen people to their true Promised Land. God promised Abraham, " the final outcome of the Day of the Lord will be that the arrogance of man will be brought low and the pride of men humbled; the Lord alone will be exalted in that day."

In the Old Testament, the word for "spirit" in Hebrew is "ruach," meaning "spirit wind or breath." In the New Testament, the Greek word for spirit" is "pneuma", also meaning "wind or breath." At the crux where Jesus encountered Nicodemus, he said. "You don't understand everything about the wind, but you see its effects. That is just how it is with the birth of the Spirit." Jesus wanted Nicodemus to know that he didn't have to understand everything about the new birth before he experienced it.

The wind is now swirling about the global atmosphere as it is sifting the planet. The profound question is, "who really understands it?" The sifting process of the "redeeming wind" is blowing through God's two corporate witnesses separating the chosen from the hour of retribution, yet "who understands?" Sadly, the rejection from the failing nominal church will make their long tragic way to their own Diaspora with having their portion with the unbelievers after missing the rapture.

With urgency, the "Lord of the Harvest" is sending out the remnant as lambs among wolves as the harvest of the earth is ripening. This is summarized in the old popular hymn from the nineteenth century called "Bringing in the Sheaves" which is based on the workers in the field. To bring in the sheaves refers to the idea that one day believers will come before the Lord, bringing others with them as their sheaves that they birthed with the Gospel. A winnowing staff or fork would scoop up what had been threshed and throw it into the wind.

The Parable of the Wheat and Tares

Matthew 13

"The kingdom of heaven is like a man who sowed good seed in his field; [25] *but while men slept, his enemy came and sowed tares among the wheat and went his way. But when the grain had sprouted and produced a crop, then the tares also appeared. So, the servants of the owner came and said to him, 'Sir, did you not sow good seed in your field? How then does it have tares?' He said to them, 'An enemy has done this.' The servants said to him, 'Do you want us then to go and gather them up?' But he said, 'No, lest while you gather up the tares you also uproot the wheat with them. Let both grow together until the harvest, and at the time of harvest I will say to the reapers, "First gather together the tares and bind them in bundles to burn them, but gather the wheat into my barn.*

It is critical to understand the eternal perspective of the coming final harvest of the world. Jesus revealed His grave concern of corruption among the kingdom community in the sifting parables in the Book of Matthew. He warned of patience for the sifting of tainted hearts and deceitful unbelievers that had to be sifted in time. When the disciples asked Jesus, why He spoke to them in parables, He answered "Because it has been given to you to know the mysteries of the kingdom of heaven, but to them it has not been given. For whoever has, to him more will be given, and he will have abundance; but whoever does not have, even what he has will be taken away from him."

The parables have been called "earthly stories with a heavenly meaning." The parable of the Wheat and the Tares was given to explain that at the end of the Tribulation, all unbelievers will be eternally separated for rejecting God and for sin and unbelief. It involves the truth of internal sifting versus eternal separation. In the parable, this was answered when the wise farmer recognized that the ultimate answer to tares among the wheat would only come at the final hour.

The heart of this parable is not how it is often portrayed. Even many commentaries use this story as an illustration of the condition of the church, noting that there are both true believers and false professors in both the prodigal church and the chosen. Jesus distinctly explains that the field is not the church; it is the world.

The practical specifics of this parable would have made a lot more sense to Jesus's original audience because of their integral knowledge of farming. Yet, the timing of the story must have been puzzling to them, because it wasn't is clear that it defined the coming "Day of the Lord." This parable clearly exposed the final hour of corruption of the world and the need for sifting. It defined the final corrupting influence of lawlessness and counterfeit faith injected that professed to be genuine even as the tares resembled authentic wheat.

In the days of Jesus, if one farmer wanted to sabotage another, it was common for a farmer to sow "bearded darnel" into the wheat field of another. This counterfeit toxic weed was called, "bearded darnel" and it mimicked many characteristics of wheat. Before they matured, the two plants were almost identical, but as they grew, the differences became apparent in the fruit. A grave difference was the darnel was poisonous and in big enough doses would kill a person. So, it's not something a farmer wants mixed up in their harvest. The concerned farmer would want to remove the darnel, but they were warned that they could mistakenly throw out perfectly good wheat. He instructs them to leave the separation to the harvesters whose job it is to remove the darnel at the end of the age.

It is ironic that in Webster's dictionary describes the saying, "to separate the wheat from the chaff" is "to decide which things or people in a group are good or necessary, and which are not. An important thing for us to understand is we are not the harvesters, but the sowers. We are compelled to keep out focus on our place of redeeming the time and our place with Him. The truth is Jesus Christ will one day establish true righteousness in the elect. After He raptures the validated church out of this world, God will pour out His righteous wrath.

The parable concludes with the process of letting the wheat and darnel both grow together until the harvest at the end of the age. We must be careful to not always try to discern between who is a weed and who is genuine. In my early years, I could have been judged by everyone to be darnel. God looks upon the heart. The Apostle Paul said the he did not even judge himself. We are not to take it upon ourselves to uproot unbelievers because the difference between true and false believers isn't always obvious. Tares, especially in the early stages of growth, resemble wheat, likewise, a false believer may resemble a true believer. The caution given is the wheat and tares cannot be safely sifted while they are growing.

God's Eternal Turning Point

Now He who searches the hearts knows what the mind of the Spirit is, because He makes intercession for the saints according to the will of God. And we know that all things work together for good to those who love God, to those who are the called according to His purpose. For whom He foreknew, He also predestined to be conformed to the image of His Son, that He might be the firstborn among many brethren.

One of my experiences with sowing seed has never left me. I had an incarcerated young man that was taught from thirteen to be an assassin for the Mexican Mafia by his father. He was tattooed like a billboard for the devil and one morning in church, he cried out to surrender to Jesus from his torturous gang life. For a month, I watched him grow like a weed until he stood staring at me with tears through my office door as I called him into my office.

In agony, he confessed to me that he could not be a Christian. His face spoke volumes to me as I said," Well, it's a little late for that," trying to lift his heart. He responded by saying that he had gone way too far in his life and God could never forgive him. I was stunned by his despair and silently pleaded to the Lord for the right thing to say. I responded by saying, "Son, do you often offend God like that?" He quickly said, "Pastor, you know me better than that, I'm afraid of Him." I then told him, "Well son, you just did." I intensely asked him the next question, "Do you really believe that your sin is more powerful than the blood of Jesus?" I then witnessed the years of guilt and chains fall to the floor.

The most often question I have gotten from hurting kids over the years is, "If God is so good, if He is so almighty, then why is there so much evil in the world?" This is a profound question, and it arises in every heart, in every generation, but now the gravity of the question is more desperate but the answer from Jesus is the same, to the point, "What good is it for someone to gain the whole world, yet forfeit their soul?

CHAPTER ELEVEN

The Coming Hour of Trial for Israel

Ephesians 5

For you were once darkness, but now you are light in the Lord. Live as children of light and find out what pleases the Lord. Have nothing to do with the fruitless deeds of darkness, but rather expose them. It is shameful even to mention what the disobedient do in secret. But everything exposed by the light becomes visible, and everything that is illuminated becomes a light. [14] This is why it is said:

> "Wake up, sleeper,
>
> rise from the dead,
>
> and Christ will shine on you."

Be very careful, then, how you live, not as unwise but as wise, making the most of every opportunity, because the days are evil. Therefore, do not be foolish, but understand what the Lord's will is.

I am very sad over how little most Christians know about their silent partner Israel. It is time to stop looking into our pockets and start looking into our heart, redeeming the time and getting a grip on the twin plight of Israel. The fretful journey home for Israel is not about location; it is about dislocation. We will see later how the Lord dislocated Jacob's thigh to cause him to lean on his staff for the rest of his life. Israel has entered into the concluding wars will to lead them to lean on their Messiah just as the nominal church is in civil war and dislocation.

To redeem something is to buy it back, and to regain possession of it. Time is a great gift from God, and none of us know how many seconds remain, only God knows. He wants us to live in constant awareness of the ticking clock and "to redeem the time, the more we see the day approaching." Unfortunately, the only ticking our young people are listening to is "TikTok. As Paul warned, no good soldier gets entangled in the affairs of civilian life. We are to be ambassadors to those lost and to Israel in this grazing maze.

The same bell that rings from history is now tolling with the epic warning that had tormented Israel through the Diaspora as they were engulfed in desperation with no identity. The closing hours of this present evil age are now the tragic reprint of the same horrid hatred for Israel. War and terrorism are now climaxing again, even in our nation, to drive Israel into the sea.

Jesus has always deeply loved Israel through the ages with the truth, but He knew their redemption could only be received through the portals in His hands. They still long for eternal comfort yet in their pride they still ignored the promise their Messiah gave as He faced the cross. He assured the remnant that "the Comforter, which is the Holy Spirit, whom the Father will send in my name, shall teach you all things, and bring all things to your remembrance." This promise shifted the eternal axis of time in a world separated from their Creator. He suspended time as He imparted eternity into His disciples with the Wind at Pentecost. If only the rest of Israel would have not resisted the Holy Spirit, where would they be?

As we look today, the most volatile thirty-five acres on planet earth are in Jerusalem, known as the Temple Mount, on which the ancient Jewish Temples of Israel once stood. Both the Old and New Testament affirm that a new Temple will once again occupy the former ground as part of God's end time purpose for the nation of Israel. Yet, will it be their greatest blessing or their greatest curse?

The three major world religions of Judaism, Christianity, and Islam have battled for this site for more than one thousand years. The Islamic temple, the Dome of the Rock, now has precedence over the entire area as the committed Jewish people anxiously awaiting resolution to be able to rebuild their Temple upon this original site. A prominent declaration is that there is no room to rebuild the Temple, yet the Book of Revelation speaks of a final different solution. It is hidden and engraved in God's Word.

The saddest days of the Jewish calendar are the Nine days of Av when the destruction of the Holy Temples are remembered. These tragedies include the destruction of the first Temple by Solomon being destroyed by Babylon and the second Temple by Herod destroyed by Rome. Jesus warned Israel that their priority for a Temple would become greater than their desire for their Messiah. Every sincere orthodox Jewish believer in Jerusalem today proclaims no rest until this sorrow is released by a rising new Temple. The tragedy is this unlearned lesson will repeat, leading to opening the door to a counterfeit Messiah.

In Jerusalem stands one remaining wall around the Old Temple Mount site today where Jewish people slip their written prayers into the wall to plead for their own personal desires. It was nicknamed "the Wailing Wall" due to other nations witnessing the Jewish people crying and praying over it. It is a tragic "selfie" of Israel continuing to wander the spiritual desert despairingly searching for the clues they already have.

This retaining wall was built to protect the Temple. Today, it doesn't protect anything, yet it is the only place where the Jewish people are allowed to even congregate. Like most religious artifacts it is merely a token symbol of the genuine article. It is assumed that the Western Wall is a place for peace and happiness but think again. In fact, it has become the womb of long memories of suffering and prayers for restoration.

Jesus the Messiah has travailed in their birth, waiting for their repentance through brokenness since He declared, "It is finished!" Tragically, Israel has refused to follow Him and have chosen to be self-determined in their own strength. Their strong will has carried them into one gauntlet after another, as the feckless world taunts them as the evil ones. The real answer for Israel will not be made from stone, because the problem is the corporate heart of stone that continues to reject their Messiah. There is a desperate need for Israel to be revived from the breath of the Holy Spirit. This is at the core of why they have never been able to fulfil the law or to be the witness they were created to be. At least, not yet.

The Beginning Deep Trouble of Jacob

Genesis 32

That night Jacob got up and took his two wives, his two female servants and his eleven sons and crossed the ford of the Jabbok. After he had sent them across the stream, he sent over all his possessions. So, Jacob was left alone, and a man wrestled with him till daybreak. When the man saw that he could not overpower him, he touched the socket of Jacob's hip so that his hip was wrenched as he wrestled with the man. Then the man said, "Let me go, for it is daybreak." But Jacob replied, "I will not let you go unless you bless me." The man asked him, "What is your name?" "Jacob," he answered, Then the man said, "Your name will no longer be Jacob, but Israel, because you have struggled with God and with humans and have overcome."

"The heart of the human problem is the problem of the human heart."
  Oswald J. Smith

The heart of the problem of Israel can be traced all the way back to the heart of the original patriarch Jacob. The name "Jacob" defines him graphically in his carnal nature mixed with his faith. From the Hebrew, Jacob (Ya'aqov) means "to follow from behind, to supplant or to overreach" and it leads to the Hebrew word for "heel." All of these descriptions paint the intricate picture of Jacob from birth. He depicts all of us from traveling from being called to being chosen.

Jacob came out of the womb with his twin brother Esau, holding onto his heel. It is mystifying how he even wrestled from the womb with a desperation to be the "firstborn with the double inheritance." This continued when he conspired with his mother to deceive his father Isaac to give him the blessing through deceit. Later, Jacob disguised himself as his brother and stole his birthright. Esau then discovered this from his father, and Jacob ended up having to flee from him into the desert which led to his final breaking.

At this point, when Esau was gaining on him, Jacob sent a parade of gifts to win him over before their confrontation. The only thing greater than Jacob's fear was his manipulation. This continued his patterned heart issue with bartering with God and with Esau, trying to accomplish the Lord's will in his own strength.

Before his confrontation with Esau, Jacob sets up camp for the night expecting the wrath of his brother. But instead, without warning, a mysterious man appears out of nowhere to wrestle with him. After many hours, the aggressor reaches down and wounds his thigh where he will have to lean on a staff for the rest of his life. After wrestling through the night, Jacob receives the revelation that this mysterious person is actually God Himself. In his brokenness, Jacob called this place Peniel and said, "It is because I saw God face to face, and yet my life was spared." Even today, Israel doesn't understand that they are not wrestling with flesh and blood.

The next morning, the Lord asked Jacob his name, as if He didn't know. He said to him, "Your name will no longer be Jacob, but Israel, because you have struggled with God and with humans and have overcome." The name Israel in Hebrew origin is derived from "Yisrael," meaning that **"God perseveres."** This rings throughout the heritage of the seed of Abraham and will not end until the Valley of Decision.

Jacob had to come to the end of himself to discover that true faith is a repentant faith. Even in that, Jacob would have to lean on a staff of the promise of a fulfilment in the Messiah. He saw through the glass darkly that by turning from self-reliance, we find rest in salvation. The Apostle Paul warned of falling short of this coming rest for the Hebrews with a bizarre statement. He said, "For he that is entered into his rest, he also hath ceased from his own works, as God did from his. Let us labor therefore to enter into that rest, lest any man fall after the same example of unbelief." As I mentioned before unbelief is the opposite of faith which is "to trust in, to cling to, and fully rely upon the Lord God and not your own understanding."

As Jacob, the fact is that our real struggle is not against our own flesh and blood which is forgotten by many Christians like Jacob. The Apostle Paul did not call the believer to enter into spiritual warfare because we should already be in the middle of it and not drifting in the desert of unbelief. Like Jacob, we have to realize we have all been in a spiritual battle from the womb. Life was hard for Jacob because Jacob was very hard. He was a dreadful pioneer of the faith, but aren't we all. If you are ignoring that fact, you are already defeated.

The Apple of His Eye

Zechariah 2

"Come, Zion! Escape, you who live in Daughter Babylon!" For this is what the LORD Almighty says: "After the Glorious One has sent me against the nations that have plundered you, for whoever touches you touches the apple of his eye, I will surely raise my hand against them so that their slaves will plunder them. Then you will know that the LORD Almighty has sent me.

I am still enamored by the birth of my youngest son. As he was about to surface the chord was wrapped on him causing his vital sins beginning to disappear which set in panic. When he surfaced, he appeared to be still born because his color was gray. Suddenly, he gasped and little circle of pink came over his heart area. As he took a gasp one by one, the pink flowed through his little body. All of a sudden, without crying, he opened his littles little eyes that spoke, "what is going on?" I had never been so excited to see someone's eyes in my life.

If we could only see ourselves as God sees us, our journey would be peaceful rest with blessed assurance. This leads to the Biblical origin of the phrase "the apple of my eye" which refers to the pupil of the eye. In ancient times. the pupil was already understood to be the small round center of the eye comparable to an apple. Since the pupil is essential to vision it was considered to be precious and needed to be protected at any cost. This symbolizes the Lord's cherishing love and protection for God's chosen people.

The apple of your eye is translated in Hebrew, "the little man of the eye." When you look into someone's eye, you can see yourself reflected in the pupil of their eyeball as a little person. It concedes the great intimacy and deeper love that God has for every one of his children. The most profound reflection of Israel came through the very Son of God at the cross. Yet, instead of protecting him at all costs, the Father had to look away for the reflection from our sin. This is a great mystery still hidden from most of Israel to this very day.

Israel appears to be either a grave mystery or a travesty, even to the Christian today. Israel has always been held by God to a higher standard because they were called out be the teacher to the nations. Tragically, they fell over and ended up being taught their ways. I agonize that the prodigal church is also repeating their same history. Jeremiah warned all of us that, "whatever is right in your own eyes without realizing that leads to death." This what happens when we when perceive through the lens of this present evil age.

The relationship between Jacob and Esau is now a reflection between Israel and the nominal church. There is a "sibling rivalry and a grave distance from brotherhood with a spirit of antagonism from both the sides. As these two brothers, there has been wrestling from the womb with controversy until a threat comes. We are witnessing this taking place at this moment as we wake up that we have the same adversary. This world is not the friend of Israel or the church. This brings the warning to love them from a cautious distance and to not be unequally yoked with unbelievers.

The prophet Zechariah said, "He who touches you touches the apple of My eye." In other words, anyone who harms Israel is harming God. I am astonished by the twisted slaves possessed by evil and their own ignorance. They are blind to history and the presence of God. Their dark conspiracy of "antisemitism" is not their own but from Satan himself. They now declare Israel and our nation as Satan and the great Satan as their fruit is only blind hatred.

The Messiah's patience is about to run out and the globe and its rebels will soon see who truly is the "apple of God's eye in living and dying color. The myth that you can destroy a person or a nation "in the name of God" is beyond blasphemy. They will be shattered when the Messiah parts the skies with His vengeful sword.

The Cataclysmic Troubles of Jacob

Jeremiah was known as the "weeping prophet" for a good reason. This prophet had witnessed the harlotry of the nation he loved as they spurned their Lord. Jeremiah had "fire in his bones" over the agony of the sinfulness of Israel. He became the voice for God to this unrepentant people. Israel refused the warnings from Jeremiah over and over and many times mocked him as the messenger of God. He finally warned the people, "After this manner will I ruin the pride of Judah, and the great pride of Jerusalem." God refers to them as "evil people who refuse to hear His words, as they walk in the imagination of their heart, and walk after other gods."

Eventually, through the prophet Jeremiah, the Lord promised that, one day in the future that He would bring Israel back to their homeland to begin their recovery, but their breaking would proceed in terror, involving horrific distress. Jeremiah declared that "in all history there has never been such a time of terror." Essentially, the time of Jacob's trouble corresponds to the same time period called the Great Tribulation. The global conditions will be far worse than any time in history, and humanity will be brought to the brink of self-annihilation. As part of the deliverance, the Lord says He will destroy the nations who held Judah and Israel in captivity, and He will never again allow Jacob to be completely destroyed.

Today, Israel is mostly a secular nation, except for the orthodoxy in Jerusalem. There is a respect for the Bible as a book of history of Israel's national identity, but there has not been true national repentance returning to the Lord. Israel is fermented with a nominal faith just as the prodigal church. As the birth pains of war continue under the vicious hand of terror, Israel continues to experience even greater tribulation.

During "the troubles of Jacob," Israel will face its greatest seduction by the final "Caesar." After seducing them with the promise of "peace and security, the Antichrist will entice them with the bargaining chip of a rebuilt Jewish Temple. He then props himself up as the messiah through the "Abomination of Desolation," as he falsely resurrects, mocking Christ. He then demands all their worship through his brand of his marking in fear and dominance.

This consummates their final breaking as Israel flees to the mountains abandoning Jerusalem praying for deliverance. The Lord Himself provides their rescue in the Valley of Megiddo. The Lord says He will destroy the nations who held Judah and Israel in captivity, and He will never again allow Jacob to be completely destroyed. The "time of Jacob's trouble" will demonstrate that God keeps His promises, judges sin, and saves those who trust in Him as their Messiah.

The details of the deliverance in Israel are established in the Book of Zechariah and the Book of Revelation. A key verse describing the exodus of the future remnant of Israel in Zechariah is, "I will pour out on the house of David and the inhabitants of Jerusalem a spirit of grace and supplication. They will look on me, the one they have pierced, and they will mourn for him as one mourns for an only child, and grieve bitterly for him as one grieves for a firstborn son." Israel finally deserves the name change from Jacob as the Lord makes His home in their hearts.

The Remnant from the Troubles of Jacob

Romans 11

I ask then: Did God reject his people? By no means! I am an Israelite myself, a descendant of Abraham, from the tribe of Benjamin. God did not reject his people, whom he foreknew. Don't you know what Scripture says in the passage about Elijah, how he appealed to God against Israel: "Lord, they have killed your prophets and torn down your altars; I am the only one left, and they are trying to kill me"? And what was God's answer to him? "I have reserved for myself seven thousand who have not bowed the knee to Baal." So too, at the present time there is a remnant chosen by grace. And if by grace, then it cannot be based on works; if it were, grace would no longer be grace.

The concept of the remnant of Israel was present from the very beginning of Israel's history, but it only became clearly evident with Elijah the prophet. Elijah thought he was the only person in Israel who did not bow his knee before Baal, but God told him otherwise: the remnant of Israel at that time comprised seven thousand who followed God. This has been consistent throughout the sifting and maturity of Israel. The last stage will finally launch when the remnant of the church is removed at the gate of the Tribulation.

It is graphically clear in the complete counsel of scripture that the specific events during the end times concerning Israel are about their redemption. Under their great persecution, they will be saved from destruction by their returning Messiah. Salvation and deliverance in the Old Testament are closely related, but not always inclusive. If I had one question that I could ask the Apostle Paul it would be, "How will all Israel be saved"? The question comes in with whether the Apostle Paul meant eternal salvation in the eleventh chapter of Romans or was the context about salvation from sin.

Some have read this to mean that every Israelite who is living will be eternally saved in the end. Paul taught that salvation can only come by God's grace through faith in Christ. There is already a remnant of Jewish believers, as in any culture while their nation had thoroughly and totally rejected God. Right now, our nation is a perfect example. Would the Lord extend salvation to those who actively ignore Him merely based on their ethnicity? This same question can be asked to the prodigal nominal church.

The remnant of Israel in Hebrew (שְׁאֵרִית יִשְׂרָאֵל) is a term denoting the belief that the future of Israel would be assured by the faithful remnant that will befall the cataclysmic departure from the will of God. This is a concurrent theme from the beginning with Enoch and the first rapture to the arriving one. The prophets foretold almost continually, the continuing exile and destruction of Israel, yet on the other hand, they always held the hope and promise of its survival and eternal rescue.

The truth of an overcoming remnant always resolves the point and purpose. This was a perpetual theme referenced by most of the prophets. The prophet Jeremiah spoke for the Lord, "and I will gather the remnant of my flock out of all the countries whither I have driven them and will bring them back to their folds, and they shall be fruitful and multiply." Joel promised, "For in Mount Zion and in Jerusalem there shall be those that escape and among the remnant those whom the Lord shall call."

It is the prophet Isaiah, however, where it is found in its most graphic way that greatly affected Israel's thoughts about the future. In the tenth chapter of Isaiah there is repeated statement of fact, "a remnant shall return, even the remnant of Jacob." Isaiah's concept of the remnant included both the faithful minority and those who would accept God's message under the impact of the forthcoming disaster.

The question about Israel's status as a nation permeates the letter to the Romans. Israel's status is particularly summarized by Paul where he focuses on the fact that Israel's judgment is neither total nor final. Yet Paul makes a distinction between natural and ethnic Israel, the physical descendants of Abraham, and spiritual Israel, those who share the eternal faith of Abraham. The remnant that are chosen by grace obviously refers to a remnant from among the natural descendants of Abraham who are also spiritual descendants. Israel will have its Promised Land in the coming millennium. The nation wasted by centuries of wandering, weariness, and warfare will realize her appointed represented destiny and enjoy her rightful possessions and position at last.

As we have witnessed the end of the Diaspora pour into the concurring "Aliya" (return), we will see the end of Israel's beginning. Today, many organizations, both Jewish and Christian are bringing Jewish people "home" from all countries of the world. Most are motivated by a misunderstood understanding that when all Jewish people are back in the land of Israel, the Kingdom will be established. If one takes the Scriptures literally, then there can be no Messianic Age or Kingdom without the Messiah personally present to call forward the final assembly of His people.

In this hour, we should be praying that the fullness of Israel repents, and that the hardened heart of Israel is melted by the voice of their Messiah. We must put away any conceit or presumption over Jewish unbelievers, but realize that God is aiming to also save them through His salvation. For now, let us give ourselves to prayer and to the great work of gathering the fullness of Israel through loving them with the truth.

CHAPTER TWELVE

The Coming Hour of Trial for the Church

Hebrews 5

We have much to say about this, but it is hard to make it clear to you because you no longer try to understand. In fact, though by this time you ought to be teachers, you need someone to teach you the elementary truths of God's word all over again. You need milk, not solid food! Anyone who lives on milk, being still an infant, is not acquainted with the teaching about righteousness. But solid food is for the mature, who by constant use have trained themselves to distinguish good from evil.

"No creature strays more easily than a sheep; none is more heedless; and none so incapable of finding its way back to the flock, when once gone astray: it will bleat for the flock, and still run on in an opposite direction to the place where the flock is: this I have often noticed."   Clarke

There has been a grave history traced from Israel that has persistently broken the heart of God as the church today has chosen to walk the same path as Jacob. Though we suffer in pain mostly from our own choice, do we ponder the pain that the Lord must be feeling? In fact, do we understand the grief we have caused Him from our unbelief? It is apparent that many do not understand that the Lord even has feelings by the way they live. We too often have a childish sense of entitlement just to receive what He has for us, yet what do we have for Him? All God desires from us is a "broken and contrite heart so, He can shape us into His image through His Spirit.

We have just looked into the grief of Jacob being sifted to finally stand as Israel while shattering God's heart from the beginning. I am ashamed of the critical judgement of many in the nominal church that broadcast an inferior Israel. But as Jesus said, "let him without sin cast the first stone." Can we not understand that when we look in the mirror, we see Jacob?

The travesty of the waffling church age has been the same agony from Jacob after its inception. As Israel went from one captivity to the next without a clue, the corporate and the individual witness of the church has turned inward, imploding from self-interest and carnal blessing. The only difference is we are so busy going through the motions, we have missed the exit signs.

The Prodigal Son

Luke 15

Then He said: "A certain man had two sons. And the younger of them said to *his* father, 'Father, give me the portion of goods that falls to me.' So, he divided to them *his* livelihood. And not many days after, the younger son gathered all together, journeyed to a far country, and there wasted his possessions with prodigal living. But when he had spent all, there arose a severe famine in that land, and he began to be in want. Then he went and joined himself to a citizen of that country, and he sent him into his fields to feed swine. And he would gladly have filled his stomach with the pods that the swine ate, and no one gave him anything."

I had always assumed that "prodigal" just meant being lost and then found. In fact, the whole chapter of Luke Fifteen is a series of parables Jesus talked about lost things being found: lost sheep, lost coins, and a lost son. Yet, "prodigal" also means being wasteful, extravagant or living in luxury. The prodigal son was completely to blame for a wasteful, foolish living and spending. Yet, he was not to blame for the severe famine, but was afflicted by it nevertheless.

The parable of the Prodigal son is a deep expression of the prodigal church of today, following the path of Israel. This parable is often taught to be only centered on boundless mercy and forgiveness to a son to find redemption from repentance. But it is more than just a figurative father welcoming his son with open arms, it is a father with a broken heart. **The example of the Prodigal**

Son is a solemn warning of today's entitled Christian that has entered the promises of God to feed on His grace and then turns to live in the trough of this present evil age. This is a son that nearly destroyed his father for his own selfish appetite.

The prodigal son had left home to become independent and wander in a foreign land with foreign desires. In his misery, he finally came to a moment of clarity. In the midst of his rebellion and disobedience, he found himself in a pigpen of filth. He couldn't blame his father, his brother, his friends, or even the pigs. He returned to be with his father. He had been broken to be mended.

This parable exposes the oxymoron of what is termed "the unbelieving believer." This is someone who initially received the gospel of Jesus Christ, but then does not persevere to live by faith in Christ. So, what is the destiny of a nominal Christian settled in "unbelief?" The Apostle Paul warned us in the Book of Hebrews of the fate of compromised belief when he pleaded, "see to it, brothers and sisters, that none of you has a sinful, unbelieving heart that turns away from the living God, but encourage one another daily, as long as it is called today, so that none of you may be hardened by the deceitfulness of sin."

There is no way around the cross. You either embrace it and go through it or you wander around it. There is no way back without repentance. It is where you start and certainly where you must end. Jesus refused apathy and compromise. He boldly spoke "If anyone comes to me and does not hate father and mother, wife and children, brothers and sisters, yes, even their own life, such a person cannot be my disciple. And whoever does not carry their cross and follow me cannot be my disciple.

Though salvation is a free gift from Jesus Christ, a life of discipleship will cost you everything. This was exemplified by the Jewish people facing the concentration camps. When the Nazis came for pastor, Dietrich Bonhoeffer, he wrote, "It is the grace we bestow on ourselves, grace without discipleship. Costly grace is the gospel which we must build upon if we are going to endure. It is costly because it will cost a man his life, and it is grace because it gives a man the only true life." Bonhoeffer gave his life in sacrifice. His final words were "Today is the end. For me, the beginning of life."

The Complicity of the Unrepentant Prodigal Church

2 Corinthians 11

I hope you will put up with me in a little foolishness. Yes, please put up with me! I am jealous for you with a godly jealousy. I promised you to one husband, to Christ, so that I might present you as a pure virgin to him. But I am afraid that just as Eve was deceived by the serpent's cunning, your minds may somehow be led astray from your sincere and pure devotion to Christ. For if someone comes to you and preaches a Jesus other than the Jesus we preached, or if you receive a different spirit from the Spirit you received, or a different gospel from the one you accepted, you put up with it easily enough.

It truly pains me over discharging this deep burden of this solemn message exposing the final eclipse of the church age. The truth is the nominal church now wavers as the nation of Israel. It is standing outside of the same door perishing from a lack of vision, shackled to an adulterous heart. The gospel of prosperity has seduced many to believe in a cross less Christianity centering on "having it your way." The truth is that it appears to be easier holding the hammer than the nails because it is the mantra of the global rebellion, rioting in excess while drowning in it.

The current general mission of the prodigal church is void of the articles of the faith causing a spiritual pandemic of apostasy. There are so many contaminants that have seeped in from the present evil age, leaving the nominal church in a pigpen of carnality. The church, once filled with God's Word and the power of the Holy Spirit has fallen into ritual, goosebumps, and compromise. Denominational Tribalism has turned the church into a cafeteria picking and choosing everything but truth and conviction. The nominal church is perishing from a lack of vision and devoid of the Gospel.

This peril came to my door when I was deep in the mission for incarcerated kids. I was anguished that when they left, they had nowhere to go. Then one of my greatest disappointments came when I asked pastors to take in these kids when they were released. They always refused by saying that they would corrupt their kids, but the truth is many of them were their kids. At one point out of frustration, I started a missionary church in the inner city for the kids coming out of the system and off the streets.

The church grew quickly but it left the kids behind. I found myself only picking up the kids as it turned into another theater. The worship and the service flourished, but tragically we just accomplished another theater playing the same movie that was playing down the street.

In the middle of the next night, I feverishly pled with the Lord on what to do. He spoke to me four of the strangest words that I had ever heard; "glassy winged sharp shooters." Being stunned, I opened up Google and typed it in. Instantly, an article popped up that blew me away. It was a report on the California vineyards being destroyed by a bizarre insect.

These parasites would drill into the vine to do two things. They would suck out the life juices and inject a toxic virus that destroyed the vine. The only response was to cut the vine down to the stump hoping it would revive. Well, I wasn't given that option of revival. The next service I told the church that this would be our last service and to find another church with a different mission. The reaction was deep anger for all of the wrong reasons. We had failed these kids that needed a refuge from the storm for the same song.

I am amazed and saddened at hearing the continual brutal critique of wandering Generation Z in the media and even in the church. Here is one of those critiques; "they like living their lives on social media and seeing real world issues through rose-tinted glasses. The reality of Gen Z is that they are indecisive, leading them to be easily influenced by social media. Gen Z interacts with the world differently than every other generation so far, and the early access to everything only amplifies that."

The real issues are not from the seeds that they have sown. They are walking the streets of abandonment looking for love in all of the wrong places. I know them and I have discovered their brilliance and their darkness. The truth is they are distressed orphans, abandoned by the culture and even the culture of the church. Where are those reaching out to them? The brutal truth is the general church is in heart failure and has "missed the mark" by just going through the motions. It is leading to the gauntlet of the coming rapture with the majority drifting in the same current of apathy into being unprepared. That is why Paul reprimanded the Corinthian church for their desire for "bells and whistles, but never reaching out and never growing up.

The Complicity of the Unrepentant Prodigal

1 Corinthians 3

By the grace God has given me, I laid a foundation as a wise builder, and someone else is building on it. But each one should build with care. For no one can lay any foundation other than the one already laid, which is Jesus Christ. If anyone builds on this foundation using gold, silver, costly stones, wood, hay or straw, their work will be shown for what it is, because the Day will bring it to light. It will be revealed with fire, and the fire will test the quality of each person's work. If what has been built survives, the builder will receive a reward. If it is burned up, the builder will suffer loss but yet will be saved, even though only as one escaping through the flames.

that had worked for years for a company that he felt had taken him for granted. One day the owner told him of a new project that he needed to take great care of, using only the best materials. The contractor decided this would be his last project and he would do a scam and do it in the cheapest and most careless way possible. At the end of the house project, he walked in and threw the keys to the owner. The owner threw them back and said, "Welcome to your new house!" As we have been told, "we will reap what we have sown."

Paul cautioned to be very careful on how you build on the foundation of Christ. As in all building, it was about materials and cost. The choice of materials fell into the two categories of priceless and flammable. Gold, silver, and precious stones become more pure the more they are tested by fire. Wood, hay, and stubble instantly perish in flames. Paul explains that he will be saved himself as through the fire with everything he did being destroyed. The fire does not purify the worker, it tests their workmanship. It is a sobering how many people believe they are serving God, but are doing it with no care or appreciation with unworthy, perishable materials that will burn in eternal flames.

So, what is the heart of the problem and what is the source? It is not having a repentant heart and not being a living sacrifice. Pollster George Gallup contends that fewer than ten percent of Christians could be called "deeply committed." He said most of those who profess Christianity don't even know the basic teachings from the Bible and act no differently from their Christian experience. George Barna found that almost even most so-called believers read their Bible only once a week or not at all.

I grew up watching extreme social welfare enable apathy and despair in society and the individual. It has returned with a vengeance in what is called "wokeism," not just in tainted culture but the prodigal church. It disables any type of responsibility or accountability in exchange for entitlement with a loss for purpose. The nominal church of today has enacted its own subtle and debilitating way, giving a thirst for more. It has retired the idea of pursuing the image of God with a new spectator sport.

The Apostle Paul was very clear that a pastor's greatest responsibility was to the Gospel and "to equip his flock for service." The above scriptures are prefaced by Paul telling the church in Corinth as he said, "I could not speak to you as to spiritual people but as to carnal, as to babes in Christ." He had warned that no immature branch can bear fruit. They were engraved more by their culture than the Word of God and the Holy Spirit.

Ancient Greece evolved into a theatrical culture that became a central political and religious place where theatre was part of a festival from the pagan god Dionysus. The Greek theater birthed the word "hypocrisy" in a very unusual way. Greek plays were intricate with many actors, but little budget. Their solution was to hire a single actor that wore many masks with a varied voice. This was the creation of drama and deflected the character of the actor. This is a parable of our day concerning the nominal Christian hiding behind masks for a greater appearance. It is also congruent with the Greek word for sin, "hamartia" which means "to miss the mark."

The Sifting Parable of the Ten Virgins

Matthew 25

"At that time the kingdom of heaven will be like ten virgins who took their lamps and went out to meet the bridegroom. Five of them were foolish and five were wise. The foolish ones took their lamps but did not take any oil with them. The wise ones, however, took oil in jars along with their lamps. The bridegroom was a long time in coming, and they all became drowsy and fell asleep.

"At midnight the cry rang out: 'Here's the bridegroom! Come out to meet him!'

"Then all the virgins woke up and trimmed their lamps. The foolish ones said to the wise, 'Give us some of your oil; our lamps are going out.' "'No,' they replied, 'there may not be enough for both us and you. Instead, go to those who sell oil and buy some for yourselves.' "But while they were on their way to buy the oil, the bridegroom arrived. The virgins who were ready went in with him to the wedding banquet. And the door was shut.

"Later the others also came. 'Lord, Lord,' they said, 'open the door for us!'

"But he replied, 'Truly I tell you, I don't know you.'

"Therefore, keep watch, because you do not know the day or the hour."

All of Christ's parables have vivid symbolism, deep meaning, and keys to the kingdom. Jesus revealed to the disciples the mysteries of the kingdom of God that were hidden from the alien hearts of the pharisees. The parables were framed to sift those that were chosen from the hardened trap of unbelief. We will envision one of the most prolific parables of our time.

The parable of the Ten Virgins has the address to send to the present church that is facing the imminent rapture. This parable reinforces the call for readiness in the face of the uncertain time of the "coming Thief in the night". It has been defined as a "watching parable". The profound importance and the thrust of this parable is that Christ will return an unknown hour when His people must be prepared with their lamps being full. It entails the heart and soul of the awaiting believer (virgin) preparing to meet his Lord in the sky at the veiled rapture of the church (bride). I truly believe this is the most graphic portrayal of who will be taken and those that are left at the door in outer darkness. This parable is for the remnant of the hour who are being tempered at the door the Tribulation.

The Parable of the Ten Virgins is described in the setting of a first-century Jewish wedding. Normally, a bridegroom with some of his intimate friends would leave his home to go to the bride's home, where there was to be an awesome celebration, followed by a procession through the streets after nightfall. The ten virgins are the bridesmaids who have been adorning the bride, as they expect to meet the groom as he comes from the bride's house. Everyone in the procession would carry their own prepared lamp for the darkness.

The wedding celebration would consist of several days that would lead to the return to the bridegroom's house. It is obvious that the groom who is central to this parable is the Lord coming as the Messiah at the end of the age. None of the ten virgins knew exactly when the groom would arrive, and all ten eventually fell asleep when he took longer than expected to arrive. All slept, and all were awakened by the call of the bridegroom's arrival.

The question of salvation is not the subject of the message because they all are virgins. The true question is who is ready with their lamps trimmed and filled. Preparedness is the mark of faith which is a true prerequisite for entrance into the celebration of the wedding. Some stress the point is about "being alert," but notice that all the virgins were asleep, but not all had trimmed their lamp. So, what does being "unprepared" really mean? It is those entrapped in "unbelief" with a dormant faith. Preparedness will enable one to enter the kingdom at the time of the Bridegroom's unexpected arrival. Many say they are even anticipating Christ's return, but are they preparing for Him. The truth is unveiled by whether their lamp is full and burning, symbolizing the fruit of their faith in Christ.

Why were five of the virgins considered wise and the other were considered foolish? On the surface the ten bridesmaids look all alike but inwardly they were not. Today, the five foolish virgins would be those who appear to have devotion, yet their lamps are empty, because they have not filled their lives with a pure devotion. In summary, they are not preparing themselves to meet Christ, but living for the moment and not caring about the eternal future.

The Coming Sifting Rapture

1 Thessalonians 5

Now, brothers and sisters, about times and dates we do not need to write to you, for You know very well that the day of the Lord will come like a thief in the night. While people are saying, "Peace and safety," destruction will come on them suddenly, as labor pains on a pregnant woman, and they will not escape. But you, brothers and sisters, are not in darkness so that this day should surprise you like a thief. You are all children of the light and children of the day. We do not belong to the night or to the darkness.

I am about to step into a more sensitive place without having a choice. To tell you the truth, the decades I spent in the trenches with angry incarcerated kids, even threatening my life, is what prepared me to be tough enough for writing this book. It will cause a problem for some, because it doesn't have the common classic brand of appeasement. We are too far along for that. The truth is we will all be saved through fire in one way or the other, either in glory or in shame.

The Apostle Paul convicted the carnal church in Corinth about building upon their eternal faith. He cautioned that the approaching "Day" that would bring to light the testing of the quality of each person's work. As the end of the church age is about to expire, we must repel the impending darkness. Paul warns that "you know very well that the day of the Lord will come like a thief in the night. While people are saying, peace and safety, destruction will come on them suddenly, as labor pains on a pregnant woman, and they will not escape."

As the clock is approaching midnight, there is little left that has to transpire before the rapture, except the maturity of the remnant. Today, there is an invoked apathy caused by a tragic misperception. In the nominal church, it is assumed that no professing believer will be left behind at the rapture. This has caused a false narrative that will be fatally exposed at the highest price. This myth assumes that all nominal Christians will inherit an equal reward as the Apostle Paul. Our salvation is truly the eternal gift of God, yet we will all have to give an account; not for the ransom for sin, but for our faithfulness after receiving forgiveness.

This leads to the question, "what will happen if the nominal Christian is left behind?" The answer is severe discipline with mercy in the sifting tribulation. How can the Lord revoke salvation that has been paid for by the blood of His Son? He can't and he won't. Yet, how can he reward the unfaithful believer without discipline when Christ is full of both grace and righteousness. The Lord has never rewarded bad behavior. The answer here is not about heaven or hell. It is a matter of the obscure deployment over what is called "outer darkness."

"Outer darkness" is not a place of hell, it is the impending Tribulation. Specifically, "outer darkness" will be the departure of the unfaithful into the Tribulation and the awaiting sifting of their souls. Jesus uses the term "outer darkness" to describe a condition of great sorrow, and retribution. It stands in vivid contrast to the brightly lit and joyous celebration attended by those who were ready. The word "tribulation" (thlipsis) in Greek means "to crush, squeeze out compress. I truly believe that this will be how and where the foolish virgins will retrieve their lacking oil.

Also, in the parable of the Wedding Feast, the bridegroom gathers the wise virgins to the wedding with His faithful bride. Jesus uses the term "outer darkness" to describe a place of great discipline, sorrow, loss, and grief. The recipient accepted the invitation but he was tattered, torn and unprepared. He was truly redeemed, yet he was unfaithful. This is also explained in the Book of Matthew when Christ's warns that "two men will be in the field; one will be taken and the other left. Two women will be grinding with a hand mill; one will be taken and the other left. "Therefore, keep watch, because you do not know on what day your Lord will come." These were both faithful and the unfaithful servants. Paul told us "to work out our salvation with fear and trembling to be blameless and pure."

The Truth Be Told to the Preparing Remnant

Matthew 24

"But about that day or hour no one knows, not even the angels in heaven, nor the Son, but only the Father. As it was in the days of Noah, so it will be at the coming of the Son of Man. For in the days before the flood, people were eating and drinking, marrying and giving in marriage, up to the day Noah entered the ark; and they knew nothing about what would happen until the flood came and took them all away. That is how it will be at the coming of the Son of Man. Two men will be in the field; one will be taken and the other left. Two women will be grinding with a hand mill; one will be taken and the other left.

It is paramount that the Christian understands the gravity of this scripture given by Matthew. It clearly describes the condition of the generation that He returns to. This generation had vacated the Lord from their memory to indulge in the sensual leading to the perversion of the spiritual. As God sifted Noah's family as a remnant from his perverted generation, He is now sifting a remnant from the contamination of the globe and the nominal church.

The sifting process is at the core separating any harvest. We have covered the sifting of the wheat and tares and now we have seen the same with the ten virgins. As we covered earlier, Satan also tried to sift Peter from Jesus and the others disciples. This began what is among us now. The Lord has spoken often concerning a faithful remnant, and it is critical to understand the importance. As Peter said, "Dear friends, do not be surprised at the fiery ordeal that has come on you to test you, as though something strange we're happening to you."

This hour is extremely strange and difficult for the remnant contending for the faith. Practically speaking, a remnant is considered a leftover. It can be a small leftover piece of carpet, a piece of cloth, but it's always discarded and sold for a fraction of the cost. The perception of a faithful remnant is looked upon by the world as worthless. But these are priceless to the Lord has set them apart as remnants chosen by the heart of His eternal will.

So, why is a remnant mentioned constantly and given significance throughout the Bible? The prophet Isaiah expressed the importance of a remnant by saying, "Except the Lord of hosts had left us a very small remnant, we should have been like Sodom and Gomorrah." This is the other warning that Jesus gave about the generation of Noah and the one that He returns to." The elect always stand out brilliantly in the darkness like the first fruits that rise above the general harvest.

We are called to be sober and alert, "assembling together the more we see the day approaching." As Jude was surrounded by apostates, he compelled the chosen to "build up in your most holy faith and pray in the Holy Spirit, while you keep yourselves in God's love as you wait for the mercy of our Lord Jesus Christ to bring you to eternal life." He also shared to "be merciful to those who doubt; while saving others by snatching them from the fire; to others showing mercy, mixed with fear, hating even the clothing stained by corrupted flesh." If we are not preparing now, the fire in the tribulation will be the default.

Our Desperate Need for Revival

Matthew 24

At that time many will turn away from the faith and will betray and hate each other, and many false prophets will appear and deceive many people. Because of the increase of lawlessness, the love of most will grow cold, but the one who stands firm to the end will be saved.

A few months ago, I had the opportunity to speak at a facility with a large group of young men coming out of prison and recovering from addiction. At the midpoint of the service, one of the guys storm out appearing to be furious. I found out later it wasn't what it appeared to be. After the service, I met up with him to see if he was alright. As he wept, he revealed the deep conviction that his family would be taken to heaven and he would be left behind.

This had lanced the wound that had built up over years from denial. In truth, this exemplified the term for "putting off the Day of Evil."

A call to arms is a summons to prepare for battle. If you are someone with an unclear idea about what spiritual warfare is, then you likely have the narrow perspective of a spectator, especially in these days. How would it change your view towards spiritual battle, if you had the revelation that it was not just a war of the unseen realm, but also a war that is battling within you? In life, our faith can be tested to the limits of our soul as we begin to feel "what's the point?" One thing that we all have to face is the state of war that we have already reached in so many ways, because it is not going to go away. It is imperative that we let it refine our true identity in Christ.

For those who are neglecting their salvation and the Holy Spirit, your love for God will continue to become colder and colder. This fading love is not the prior warmth, living love for God and His truth that began your journey. Rather, it defers to the love of self and the love of money and pleasure. Growing cold is the major sign of death. The nominal church has had a major battle just like the church of Acts, but with the appearance of differing enemies. They are the same enemy with a differing schemes. They are now "loving us to death" with the Mystery of Lawlessness. This has led from apathy to temptation to compromise to comfort and eventually to apostasy.

The word "revival" means "to bring back to life those who have died." Spiritual revival is essential to one who has lost their "first love" and has a desperate need for fresh fire. While the Bible doesn't use the word "revival," it is detailed in the lives of God's people who surprisingly find true continual repentance. There have been times throughout history, where God who normally works in ordinary days has chosen to work in extraordinary ways.

The prophet Jeremiah declared that "the heart of man is deceitful above all things and beyond cure. Who can understand it?" There has always been a constant need of revival, a return to God and His ways with the outpouring of His power and grace. Periods of revival in the past were followed by sin and its devastation that ultimately led to another revival. Today, with the Messiah's return being imminent, this is different. We must realize that the last call of revival for the church age is now being processed through a remnant, unless you miss it. Through the ages, when God's power is unleashed through ordinary people, it awakens the hunger for God for others. This stems from a heart so filled with love for Christ, we're able to respond with ever progressing honesty for the truth.

As we are repeating the Days of Noah, do not expect a huge revival as some are professing. It will soberly be a quiet remnant, reflecting the return to the Days of Noah. The fingerprints from the Days of Noah involved four types of grave iniquities: great wickedness, evil imaginations of every kind, extreme violence, and total corruption. It is bewildering that these things are the primal leavening process in the foundation of today's global society, causing the returning eclipse of temporal madness as in the generation of Noah.

If you look and listen closely, you will discover a remnant that are living what they are professing. Instead of blending in with the fallen cultural or being entangled in profit, God's people are starting to come out of the closet, returning to God and reforming their ways.

GOD'S ETERNAL PROMISE

CHAPTER THIRTEEN
The Foundation of God's Eternal Promise

Matthew 17

After six days Jesus took with him Peter, James and John the brother of James, and led them up a high mountain by themselves. There he was transfigured before them. His face shone like the sun, and his clothes became as white as the light. Just then there appeared before them Moses and Elijah, talking with Jesus. Peter said to Jesus, "Lord, it is good for us to be here. If you wish, I will put up three shelters, one for you, one for Moses and one for Elijah." While he was still speaking, a bright cloud covered them, and a voice from the cloud said, "This is my Son, whom I love; with him I am well pleased. Listen to him!" When the disciples heard this, they fell facedown to the ground, terrified. But Jesus came and touched them. "Get up," he said. "Don't be afraid."

[8] When they looked up, they saw no one except Jesus.

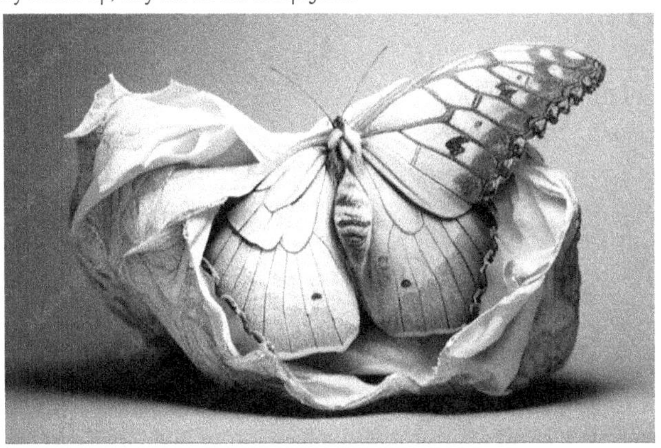

    As a teenager, I was walking along the yard when I looked down and saw a small object wiggling on the ground, when I realized it was a cocoon. I picked it up and carried it inside the house, and watched it moving for a long time. I was fascinated at the struggle that lasted for a couple of days. I finally decided to help by cracking it open, but I somehow knew it would do more harm than good. I found out later that it would have killed it. It finally broke open and found its wings. Nature has so many parables that match our experience. So many times, in our mission, I would move to help a kid and have the Spirit stop me. And later, I would see their appointed time of brokenness had not yet arrived.

The word transfiguration (metamorphoomai) means the process of "metamorphosis" which is to be transformed." Transfiguration in scripture is the beautiful process of turning the caterpillar nature into the wings of the Spirit. It enables us to mediate the message of Christ to others and to present God's loving action in the world. The true test of mature spirituality comes from obedience to perpetual repentance to Christ.

The transfiguration of Jesus Christ displayed the most inclusive demonstration of the Messiah's eternal promise to bring forth the Kingdom of Heaven with the marriage of the Old and New Covenant. This monumental revelation from heaven displayed the full redemption coming to the chosen. This incredible event prophesied the process of our salvation central to the message of the law and the prophets. It enables us to mediate the message of Christ to others and to present God's loving action to a fallen world.

Peter, James, and John were given a glimpse of heaven to strengthen them for the terrible struggles and suffering that were soon to come. The Apostle Peter was one of the three apostles who witnessed the marriage of God's promise to humanity. He was also present in the Garden of Gethsemane as Jesus prayed to the Father. He fell with his face to the ground sweating blood, and prayed, "My Father, if it is possible, may this cup be taken from me. Yet not as I will, but as you will." These two events were the bookends that profoundly impacted the devotion of His disciples concerning brokenness.

From the Mount of Transfiguration, the disciples were frozen by amazement. Suddenly, they hear the Father's voice spoke from heaven saying, "This is my Son, whom I love; with him I am well pleased. Listen to him!" When the disciples heard the Father's voice from heaven, they fell face down to the ground terrified. Jesus being aware of their fear, told them not to fear and He touched them with mercy.

Jesus then stood alone, unveiling God's redemptive plan to rescue humanity. This pronounced that the Law and the Prophets must now give way to Jesus who would replace the old way as the "new and living way." The eternal axis shifted from planet earth to the hope of heaven. but it was only available for those who will choose it.

To appreciate what's going on with the Transfiguration, you must factor in the reality that this remarkable scene had taken place just a few days after Jesus had told his disciples for the very first time that He was going to die. And when Jesus told His disciples He was going to die, they were offended. Peter, speaking for the group, grabbed Jesus and said, "far be it from you to die, it can't happen." Jesus was upset with Peter and told him, "you savor the things of man and not of God." Only God truly knows how they work together in His plan of salvation.

The Eternal Promise of All Things New

Revelation 21

Then I saw "a new heaven and a new earth," for the first heaven and the first earth had passed away, and there was no longer any sea. I saw the Holy City, the new Jerusalem, coming down out of heaven from God, prepared as a bride beautifully dressed for her husband. And I heard a loud voice from the throne saying, "Look! God's dwelling place is now among the people, and he will dwell with them. They will be his people, and God himself will be with them and be their God. He will wipe every tear from their eyes. There will be no more death' or mourning or crying or pain, for the old order of things has passed away."

We live in a world that is a "microwave culture" that wants everything to be "now and new," yet it is instantly outdated and perishable. We purchase insurance and extended warranties to protect our investments that last longer than our possessions. Being outcast from Eden, moth and rust destroy, thieves steal, everything is subject to decay, we are dust and return to the dust.

At the culmination of the Book of Revelation, the prophet John envisioned "a new heaven, a new earth" and a new Jerusalem." as hears God Almighty say, "Behold, I am making all things new." These statements are drawn from the well of Old Testament prophecies. Within the veil of God, all things are new every morning with determination and truth. God does not merely make new things to replace what is old, broken, and obsolete; he makes all things to be new for eternity. This promise transcends our current categories of temporary newness, revealing a new kind of newness that never wears out or breaks down. The Alpha and Omega makes all things new.

I not only understand the sheer gravity of the contents of this book, but I also understand its necessity. There used to be a saying that "you are so heavenly-minded that you are no earthly good. For this hour, it should be reversed by saying, "you're so worldly minded, your no heavenly good. James expressed, "you do not even know what will happen tomorrow. What is your life? You are a mist that appears for a little while and then vanishes." With the course of this present evil age, it is so difficult to not be swept away by the cares of this life. As we turn the page to our promised eternal destiny, there are a myriad of reasons we to retain them. The fundamental promises from God were authored through covenant.

THE MAJOR COVENANTS

The Noahic Covenant Genesis 9
This is a covenant God establishes with Noah after the flood in which he resets and renews the blessings of creation, reaffirming God's image in humanity and the work of dominion. This covenant promises the preservation of humanity and provides for the restraint of human evil and violence.

The Abrahamic Covenant Genesis 12
God promises Abraham a Promised Land with descendants as numerous as the stars. This blessing promised to Abraham would extend through him to all the peoples of the earth.

The Mosaic Covenant Exodus 19
This was established with the people of Israel at Mount Sinai. It provided the Law to govern and shape the people of Israel in the Promised Land.

The Davidic Covenant   2 Samuel 7
God promises a descendant of David to reign on the throne over the people of God. This covenant becomes the basis for hope of a Messiah and makes sense of the Gospels' concern to show Jesus was the rightful King of the Jews.

The New Covenant Luke 22
This was the eternally promised rescue and renewal of the exiled people of God shackled in Babylon. This was the promise that would bring forgiveness of sin, and the intimate knowledge of God.

Solomon praised that God had placed eternity in the heart of man. The Lord has His desire in His eternal Word overflowing with his promises of love, forgiveness, salvation, and hope for everyone who trusts in his Son Jesus. This alone pulls back the veil to give us a glimpse of the amazing position of eternal security, yet we must focus now to keep living before Him without wavering. God's promises throughout the ages are the foundation of our relationship tucked in the portals in His hands.

There are over seven thousand promises that God has made just to you personally, yet how many do we truly cling? In each and every promise, God has pledged that each will come to pass, because God is eternally faithful, and we can have full assurance that each will be realized. This generation has been subjected to broken promises as Jesus warned that our enemies will even come from our own households. We must pray that the Lord heals our "unbelief" and truly realize that God is far different and that He is eternally unchanging.

The Promised Eternal Destiny for Israel

Genesis 12

"Now the Lord had said unto Abram, Get thee out of thy country, and from thy kindred, and from thy father's house, unto a land that I will show thee; and I will make of thee a great nation, and I will bless thee, and make thy name great, and thou shalt be a blessing; and I will bless them that bless thee, and curse him that curseth thee, and in thee shall all families of the earth be blessed."

Four hundred years after the cataclysmic flood, a new chapter in redemption was opened when God called Abraham to be the father of a new nation. This was the beginning of what was to become the nation of Israel that would never end. This was not a conditional promise, and there is not a single scripture in the Bible anywhere that revokes it, yet it has again caused the rage of the nations. Israel has the promise of preservation and restoration as a blueprint for us to follow. It is by grace alone and it will always be.

The second promise was given to Abraham that he would be the father of many nations and that kings would descend from him. God promised him that he would inherit the Promised Land of Canaan, stretching from the Nile to the Euphrates river. The title to the land is declared to be eternal. The second promise to Abraham was more important, because the promise was spiritual. God promised Abraham that in his Seed all the nations of the earth would be blessed. There was only the exception with the horrific Diaspora when their land was repossessed until 1948. From this promise, the land will always be entitled to Israel regardless of evil foes as long as the earth endures, even through the coming millennial kingdom. The globe still continues to "kick against the pricks."

It is important to envision that the Law of Moses was not just a promise, but a declaration. Understanding the Law was a difficult problem because the point and purpose was It even misunderstood by Israel itself. Ultimately, the Law was to reveal to humanity that no one can keep the Law but everyone falls short of God's standard of holiness. That realization causes us to rely on God's mercy and grace. When Christ came, He fulfilled the Law and with His death paid the penalty for our breaking it. This most important promise was also spiritual. God promised Abraham that in his seed all the nations of the earth would be blessed. This promise come from the seed of King David, the promised Messiah, Jesus Christ. This was a type of Abraham's spiritual descendants inheriting the earth.

The underlying promise and principles of the coming prophets were given to Eve after the fall of man. Today, the Old Testament prophets still play a crucial role in redemptive history today. These prophets taught truth and interpreted the Word of God. They called the unrighteous to repentance. They were vessels for reconnecting with its consummation in the person of John the Baptist.

Now, the question of God keeping His eternal promises is a far bigger question than just a dispensational debate. The question of God keeping His promises to Israel is based on divine integrity because if God has changed His promises to Israel, we're all in a lot of trouble. Israel's very existence as a nation is tied to the promises of God without question. Yet, however, as a nation, they must now go from wandering in the desert through the tribulation period as the Lord will continue to hold their hand. As they verge upon extinction by the armies of the Antichrist, they will finally recognize Jesus Christ as their Messiah, Savior and King.

The Two Valleys of Promise for Israel

John 18

When he had finished praying, Jesus left with his disciples and crossed the Kidron Valley. On the other side there was a garden, and he and his disciples went into it. Now Judas, who betrayed him, knew the place, because Jesus had often met there with his disciples. So, Judas came to the garden, guiding a detachment of soldiers and some officials from the chief priests and the Pharisees. They were carrying torches, lanterns and weapons.

The famous twenty-third Psalm was written by King David summarizing the beautiful relationship with the Messiah. David was a former shepherd boy centered in the valley of the shadow of death. He was well acquainted not only with sheep, but also with the Lord as his shepherd. In this psalm, David encounters the Shepherd walking with him. He is comforted by knowing the Good Shepherd's rod and staff that would protect him. It sets the stage for the coming valleys leading to the mountain top. This psalm leaves both Israel and the church with hope on the path of deep trial.

Few understand that valleys in the Bible have far more meaning than just geographical markers on an ancient map. God has repurposed valleys throughout scripture as tests of faith to deepen our hope and confidence in the One who is with us in each and every valley. In the Bible, valleys are often a metaphor for difficult times, times of darkness, despair, and even defeat.

The Kidron Valley was the deepest and darkest valley in all of eternity. "Kidron" is the name for the "winter torrent" which on the eastern side of Jerusalem between the city and the Mount of Olives. Ironically, it is also the location of the return of the Messiah. Through this mountain ravine no water runs, except until the heavy rains in the mountains round about Jerusalem. It rocky banks are filled with ancient tombs, especially the left bank opposite the temple area. Ironically, it is also the location of the return of the Messiah.

After the Last Supper, Jesus crossed into this valley with his disciples into the garden of Gethsemane. Jesus crossed the Brook of Kidron. This stream was the drainage from the temple, and it would be reddish from the blood of thousands of Passover lambs as a vivid reminder to Jesus of His soon sacrifice. The promise from this valley was riddled with betrayal and desertion, but it gave way to the ultimate sacrifice and triumph in the heart of eternity.

The promise of the gospel is not a perfect life of health, wealth, and prosperity, but it is found by the believer traveling the narrow path of testing to blessing in the valleys of life. As we face terrifying conflict, consequences, and temptation, our character is built as we are sifted into the image of God. But even in the darkest valley, God is with us. Although we walk through the shadow of the valley of death, He is our shepherd.

The Valley of Dry Bones

Ezekiel 37

The hand of the LORD was on me, and he brought me out by the Spirit of the LORD and set me in the middle of a valley; it was full of bones. He led me back and forth among them, and I saw a great many bones on the floor of the valley, bones that were very dry. He asked me, "Son of man, can these bones live?"

From the Book of Ezekiel comes the anthem of redemption of Israel as they discover the ultimate power of the Holy Spirit. The Lord brings His prophet Ezekiel to a shuttering valley through an incredible vision. Ezekiel is commanded to reveal an astonishing prophecy of the future for Israel. In this valley of death and bones, there is a connection of human skeletons that become covered with flesh. God reveals these bones are truly the people of Israel. From this valley, Ezekiel envisions their resurrection that brings them back to the final true Promised Land of Israel.

This spectacular promise seems impossible in light of Israel's position in their current condition. During the Diaspora, Israel was dead as a nation, deprived of her land, her king and her Temple. So, God evidently gave Ezekiel the vision of the dry bones as a comforting prophecy for the future. God promised that Israel would arise as a mighty spiritual army from the valley of death.

No created power could have restored these human bones to life. God alone caused them to live. Skin and flesh covered these bones as the holy wind was blew upon them, restoring them to life.

This vision was to encourage the desponding Jews both of their restoration after their present and long continued dispersion. It was a clear intimation of the resurrection of the dead, and it represents the power and grace of God, in the conversion of Israel to himself. The truth is, except for exception of the prophets and a few like King David, Israel never had the residing Holy Spirit. This still has not transpired yet. Although Israel came home, for the most part, they are still spiritually dormant, and will be until the church age ends.

The Rescue in the Valley of Decision

Joel 3

Swing the sickle, for the harvest is ripe.

Come, trample the grapes, for the winepress is full,

and the vats overflow,

so great is their wickedness!"

Multitudes, multitudes

in the valley of decision!

For the day of the LORD is near

in the valley of decision.

The coming Day of the Lord will culminate as the Lion of the tribe of Judah descends into the Valley of Decision to sift Israel from the final raging assault of the unrepentant nations. The prophet Joel describes the promise of the great and terrible return of the Messiah of Israel. The setting is the last fateful journey going from the mountain to the valley.

The Mount of Olives is not just a common hill overlooking the Valley of Megiddo. It is here, where in the last hour, the possessed Antichrist will gather the world's ten evil remaining kings for the final battle over humanity in the Valley of Decision. This will finally end the Satanic assault on planet earth that brings the eternal will of God to possessing the globe. This final sifting has its end in the very heart of Israel. Armageddon will not be just a war, but the hinge pin for eternity, placing humanity before the wine vat of judgement. It will end with blood as high as a horse's bridle for a hundred and eighty miles.

In their folly and deception, they will all join together to be hopelessly defeated in assaulting Israel by the Eternal Messiah, the Lord Jesus Christ. The nation's armies will receive the sobering sword of judgment from the Messiah's mouth as it pierces Satan's heart for eternity. The one-hundred and eighty-mile valley is to become the basin for the blood of the enemies of God's people as high as a horse's bridle, in an everlasting judgment. How does the earth reach this incredible moment without realizing the myriad of warnings from God's Word that this would transpire exactly as the Bible foretold us? While we sleep, the lines of scripture are being spoken and performed before our very eyes.

There are many myths about what the world will resemble at the return of the Messiah at this global climax. Many misunderstand that the rapture transfers the globe from the present church age back to Israel in Word and in deed. As the Jewish faithful remnant will run to be hidden in the Mount of Olives, as Christ splits it like the Red Sea, they will see their redemption from their Messiah. Israel will then weep like a mother losing her child over the One whom they pierced, as the see the pierced holes in His hands.

The Promised Eternal Destiny for the Church

Matthew 26

While they were eating, Jesus took bread, and when he had given thanks, he broke it and gave it to his disciples, saying, "Take and eat; this is my body." Then he took a cup, and when he had given thanks, he gave it to them, saying, "Drink from it, all of you.

This is my blood of the covenant, which is poured out for many for the forgiveness of sins.

I tell you; I will not drink from this fruit of the vine from now on until that day when I drink it new with you in my Father's kingdom."

The promised eternal destiny of the church is written in the suffering blood of our Messiah, as He cried out, "It is finished!" The relationship of the church must flow from the cross and the truthful Spirit of God. We are called out to not be from this world but to be the "ambassadors for heaven's sake. We perish when we forsake God for pleasures sake and fit into the mold of the apostate. It is better to be hated for what is right than to be adored by what is wrong.

The first church was surrounded by hatred and fire. They were forced to live and breathe together clinging to life and to the Spirit of Christ. This produced a great beauty and a fervent witness that was manifested in the final days of the disciples. Even Peter who betrayed Jesus three times eventually was crucified upside down in his learned humility. As we've witnessed, they were all martyred except for John who lived through being boiled in oil. There is a polarizing testimony of the church in history. She either glowed in the flames from her deep suffering and conviction or she became impaled by compromise and apostasy in the dark ages.

When we look at world history, the Prince of this World has his tactics and schemes that fall into two basic categories; persecution or embracement. He began persecuting the church and soon migrated to embracing it through a counterfeit empirical theocracy. From the time of Nimrod at the Tower of Babel, humanity inspired by evil and lawlessness has tried to mix the elements of governing politics married to pagan religion to continue to gain supreme domination, and to mock the Kingdom of God.

As with the theocratic nation of Israel, it is impossible to separate the spiritual truth from the nation itself. The separation of church and state was not about protecting the state from the church. It was about protecting the church from the state. It was about freedom of religion, not freedom from religion. Our foundation was founded on Judeo-Christian values with freedom of choice. Choice authored by God is either your ultimate blessing or your greatest curse. We are on a dark path with far greater consequences from the sorcery of "selfism."

The Apostle Paul begins the eighth chapter of Romans with the promise that "there is therefore now no condemnation to those who are in Christ Jesus, who do not walk according to the flesh, but according to the Spirit. If we have received the Lord, our path ends for destruction, but must continue with conviction. This promise is fulfilled with the harvesting of the remnant church, not from the valley but the mountain top. The tumultuous valleys of tribulation preceded this coming glorious event that occurs in the twinkling of an eye. Paul then proceeds to the point that "all of creation is awaiting and anticipating the manifestation of the sons of God." This is the adoption of sons, not children.

This chapter clearly show us that what is being referred to by the term manifestation is putting off of our mortal bodies, wherein dwells our sinful nature, and the putting on glorified bodies, being fashioned after the resurrected body of Christ. This hope is inseparably related to the personal elevation at the rapture by Jesus Christ with these two events happening at the same time. Consequently, the "manifestation of the sons of God," which refers to this event is at the end of the church age.

The Eternal Promises Lost through Unrepentance

Romans 2

But because of your stubbornness and your unrepentant heart, you are storing up wrath against yourself for the day of God's wrath, when his righteous judgment will be revealed. God "will repay each person according to what they have done." To those who by persistence in doing good seek glory, honor and immortality, he will give eternal life. But for those who are self-seeking and who reject the truth and follow evil, there will be wrath and anger.

"Of all acts of man repentance is the most divine. The greatest of all faults is to be conscious of none." Thomas Carlyle

We are often taught that God's promise is always about the future, but that is short sighted and unscriptural in many cases. We have been told that we must take the good with the bad. The truth is we must separate the good from the bad. His purpose can only be achieved through the sifting process of repentance.

The ominous issue of repentance is the most disastrous obstacle obstructing the promises of God as He waits upon us. Repentance is the deep change of heart and the new way of relating to God about sin, holiness, and about doing His will. One must be grieved by how offensive and grieving sin is to God, not simply afraid of God's retribution for your sin. True repentance is prompted by "godly sorrow," far more than saying you're sorry. All of salvation, including repentance and faith, is a result of God drawing us, opening our eyes, and changing our hearts. God's longsuffering leads us to repentance. No one can repent unless God grants repentance.

The foundational causes of the deluge in the Days of Noah were provoked by two of the gravest sins; that every inclination of the thoughts of the human heart were continual evil, and a divorcing generation that rejected God by refusing repentance. The fruit of Noah's day was equally complimented by the days of Sodom and Gomorrah. This triggered the fire from heaven as the generation was completely compromised. Lot sat daily at the gate of Sodom as a foul attorney for the "deep state" of Sodom. That night deviant sexual sinners intruded to rape the warning angels as Lot tried to save his own skin by ransoming his daughters in their place. In their retreat, Lot's wife became a pillar of salt for looking back at what she loved.

This is the parable of why our nation, the nominal church, and the globe reels on its axis as we now "play the Harlot" even more emphatic than the generation of Noah. It's time to stop the hollow music and the immoral dancing because we are exposed as spiritually poor, naked, and blind. Our identity in this generational hour is wrenching as the Messiah stands outside the door knocking. He has come quickly to judge with the blade of the awaited vengeance that is crying from under the altar.

I am sobered by the greatest example of trial through fire that defines the Old Covenant. Most of Israel is still tragically trying to find its way from vacillating in unbelief since the parting of the Red Sea. As Paul emphasized the "irrevocable" nature of Israel's calling as a nation, the trial has been relentless. Regardless of Israel's current state of unbelief, a future repentant remnant is about to fulfill their calling to establish righteousness by faith.

In contrast, our nation has repented from devotion to God into the hands of the global elites with their merchandisers at every street corner of the temple. We now have the face of our nation scarred by traitorous politicians and pillow prophets ravaging the nominal church with the same excess of rebellion for the very same reasons. This is why Jesus was forced to braid a whip.

Through spiritual lawlessness, the love of most in our nation have grown ice cold through pretension. Unrepentance is the issue for the many professing believers who will share their portion with the unbelievers. Intimacy with God is always available, but it only at the gate of confession and repentance. It is as accessible to you as God's promises. And God's invitation to you to enjoy intimate fellowship with him is that thing that is putting your faith to the test more than anything. The reality is if the church doesn't repent, the nation never will.

Do you have a repentant heart or a heart that is desperately wicked. Only daily repentance will keep you refined, keeping the fire burning. We choose everyday who we will serve, "whether it be God or the devil." As the Apostle Paul told the nominal church in Corinth, it is about the simple and pure devotion to God. It is time to stop playing church and find our knees. Don't trust the process, trust the Messiah. My deepest prayer for this last chapter is that this message for this hour will lead you into your own "Valley of Decision." As we are witnessing the current into the imminent Tribulation, we must fall into the arms of the Christ, the Author and Finisher of our faith, holding forth the Word of Life.

CHAPTER FOURTEEN

Keeping His Word

For the word of God is alive and active. Sharper than any double-edged sword, it penetrates even to dividing soul and spirit, joints and marrow; it judges the thoughts and attitudes of the heart. [13] *Nothing in all creation is hidden from God's sight. Everything is uncovered and laid bare before the eyes of him to whom we must give account.*

"Generals always prepare to fight the last war, instead of the one in front of them." Georges Clemenceau

Many years ago, a pastor had this sobering statement. "For the last fifty years, America has been cursed with blessing. Now, He has begun to bless us with cursing." The landscape of our human journey has now been blessed with cursing to find our eternal redemption and full sonship back to the Father. The Apostle Paul reiterated this trauma when he "wept with tears over those that became enemies of the cross, and declared their God was their senses." Yet in his own life's peril, he cried out, "who shall deliver me from this body of sin and death!" These bookends of agony capture the continual fall of humanity under the spell of unbelief as the anthem and the depth of our present struggle.

I am grieved over the Biblical illiteracy of the nation and the church today. It takes God's living word to diagnose the condition of man's heart with a surgical precision. Paul mandated Timothy to "present yourself to God as one approved, a worker who does not need to be ashamed and who correctly handles the word of truth." He employed Timothy to engrave the Word upon his heart to approve him, not just for service, but to God. "Approve" in Greek means "to be tried by fire." God meets us by the Holy Spirit as He works powerfully through His word. When the word of God exposes our weakness and unbelief, it demonstrates its awesome inherent power, sharpness, and accuracy.

When Paul had addressed the timid Hebrew Christians, he expressed they were too ready to follow in the failure of the children of Israel and to abandon their living faith. They were hiding from persecution with no resolve to do battle. Paul exposed that "all things are naked and open to the eyes of Him to whom we must give account." There is no one hidden before God. He sees our heart and knows how to touch and mend it, and we must give account for how we respond to His touch.

At the end of my father's life, he shared some brutal things with me from World War Two that crushed my innocence, yet it made me realize the gravity of warfare. He recollected one morning when his captain called the platoon together and he announced that he caught the guard on duty asleep in their foxhole. He warned them, "Trust me, this will not happen again!" The next week in the foxhole at night my dad was suddenly awakened by gunfire. In panic, he ran over to see the captain standing with a gun above the dead soldier that had fallen asleep. My father said that was the last time someone fell asleep on guard duty.

A graphic truth in battle is that apathy will get you killed. In warfare, battles are fought on different fronts, for different reasons, and with varying degrees of intensity. Right now, the temperature of the present spiritual war is close to insufferable as we face the hour of trial descending as a dark angel. It seems intangible, but this is a gift from God for seeking out the remnant. The remnant is veiled within the end-time church to stand as a light of the earth, "that he might present it to himself a glorious church, not having spot, or wrinkle, or any such thing; but that it should be holy and without blemish" This is certainly not the nominal church of apathy and compromise and there is no doubt that, with us or without us, the Lord will rapture His church on earth.

Paul tells us that all of our warfare is combating the schemes of the devil. At the end of the day, it is completely irrelevant if the particular opponent we face is a principality, a power, or a ruler of the darkness of this age. There is no weaponry given for those who are retreating. What soldier has ever gone into battle without a weapon or protection? The description of our weaponry in Ephesians Six, only has one offensive weapon, the Word of God.

If we are not secured and inspired by the Holy Spirit through Scripture, then we are unarmed and just a target. Paul was deeply enamored by the Bereans that stood in the courage of convictions. They were impassioned through noble character and they received the word with eagerness, yet they searched the scriptures daily whether those things the apostle shared were accurate. They had a "simple and pure devotion" to their Lord. He understood you can only keep your word when you keep His.

The Messiah has enlisted us to fight the good fight against this hideous invasion from the foul birds in the air. They say the hardest thing to teach a soldier is to "move toward the sound of battle. Even in World War Two, most soldiers never fired their rifle. The life of a nominal Christian has been turned into being a spectator sport. We are in the most ferocious war, not a traveling circus. The Apostle Paul asked Timothy, "Join with me in suffering, like a good soldier of Christ Jesus. No one serving as a soldier gets entangled in civilian affairs, but rather tries to please his commanding officer."

In warfare, there are only two options; to deny it or to embrace it. Paul prescribes them specifically in the Book of Ephesians; "Therefore put on the full armor of God, so that when the day of evil comes, you may be able to stand your ground, and after you have done everything, to stand firm with the belt of truth buckled around your waist, with the breastplate of righteousness in place, and with your feet fitted with the readiness that comes from the gospel of peace.

The "dark glass" of the sorcery of "selfism" has tainted and excluded every generation since the last world war. The mystifying lawlessness has imprisoned the planet by the deceit of the final global war. The choice for liberty is about to be vacated for the gallows of rebellion. There is no time left to put off the Day of Evil.

Standing Your Ground

2 Corinthians 4

Therefore, we do not become discouraged. Though our outer self is [progressively] wasting away, yet our inner self's being [progressively] renewed day by day. For our momentary, light distress is producing for us an eternal weight of glory beyond all measure surpassing all comparisons, a transcendent splendor and an endless blessedness! So, we look not at the things which are seen, but at the things which are unseen; for the things which are visible are temporal just brief and fleeting but the things which are invisible are everlasting and imperishable. AMP

"If you love wealth greater than liberty, the tranquility of servitude greater than the animating contest for freedom, go home from us in peace. Crouch down and lick the hand that feeds you, and may posterity forget that ye were once our countrymen. Samuel Adams

In 1776, Samuel Adams gave a convicting speech in Philadelphia chastising a group of Americans who had sided with the Crown of England. This is what inflamed and catalyzed the heart for the faithful in the American Revolution. The Patriots were inspired by faith and republican ideology as they rejected the monarchial aristocracy to stand for liberty and justice against the betraying patronizing Loyalists. Declaring independence was about severing the lethal compromise to the monarchy and the state church to return to the ultimate dependence upon their Master. We have returned to the same battlefield without the fervor of loyalty.

This cry for liberty was extended by the quote, "the tree of liberty must be refreshed from time to time with the blood of patriots and tyrants." These tyrants were the traitors that followed them through the ocean. They knew them well as the swamp who exercised dominance for their own selfish gain. This was the first declaration of war that defined the true meaning of "the separation of church and state." It was to protect the church from the state. At this point, the Patriots clearly understood that the greater enemies were those among them that sold their soul for profiteering and merchandizing. Tragically, this has resurfaced in our nation and the nominal church as many have returned "as a dog to its vomit."

They have also returned, filling the halls of the capital and the pulpits of the nominal church like Judas sat at the table of the last supper, denying and justifying his betrayal. Judas claimed he loved Jesus yet he hated the purpose of the coming cross because he felt it would not defeat the Romans or the Pharisees. Instead, Judas joined their satanic conspiracy exposing that it was actually "all about him." This brand of betrayal always comes with a kiss and "thirty pieces of silver." Satan then used the possessed Judas to destroy the completion of the mission to unleash a final assault, although his moronic act completed the kingdom of God as the Messiah cried out, "It is finished!"

The inspired patriots understood that this life is only worth living for when you discover what is worth dying for. That is why the faithful Patrick Henry proclaimed "Give me liberty or give me death!" They had bled in battle from the courage of their convictions as the new disciples that were witnessing to the truth. If we neglect the truth without protest the boot will be on our neck. If we allow the continual erosion of our Constitution to continue, the Bible will be next. In fact, this is already in motion.

John Adams said this statement "Our constitution was made only for a moral and virtuous people. It is wholly inadequate to govern any other." This truly speaks to the heart of the problem. Today, even the nominal Christian no longer seeks the liberty derived from the cross and has become its enemy. The words of Samuel Adams were a reprint of faithful Joshua as he proclaimed at the gate of the Promised Land, "If serving the Lord seems undesirable to you, then choose for yourselves this day whom you will serve." The masses of America have now chosen self-service. We would rather go to Burger King to "have it our way, so we can rule." The Apostle Paul declared that only "where the Holy Spirit is Lord, there is liberty." You can't have it both ways. From dread, they feverishly hide in the darkness. They are not only bewildered by the signs of the times, they are chasing the wind and beating the air forgetting their countrymen.

Our political arena has also returned us to the coliseum of Rome, slaughtering the innocents with lies and hatred. This has possessed the global tyrannical elites, fleeced in their lawless deception to engulf the nation with a vile thirst for power. We have been driven now in a spiritual civil war over the soul of our nation and the prodigal church. The truth is we have let them drive us from the back of the wagon looking for handouts.

The only solution is to stop allowing the branding from these tyrants and follow the Messiah. I caution you to not get obsessed with the global chessboard because it only has pawns until the violent, counterfeit king makes his final move. Keep your eyes on the King above. The Apostle Paul warned, "Jews demand signs and Greeks look for wisdom, but we preach Christ crucified: a stumbling block to Jews and foolishness to Gentiles, but to those whom God has called, both Jews and Greeks."

As this mysterious sifting is taking place, it is happening within the remnant of Israel, the nation and the church. It is having an impact on every Christian and Jew present on the globe as the blade severs the harvest, closing the church age. If you blink, you will miss it. There is a dual sifting taking place between those who refuse the cross, and those who will be removed at the rapture. It is solemnly written: "every knee will bow before me; every tongue will acknowledge God."

Truthfully, I am not as concerned about the globalist traitors in our capital or those behind the pulpit fleecing the flock as I am for the lambs that are clueless of why the razor is on their back. That is why I still haven't left the trenches. It may sound odd, but I am deeply in prayer for a reprieve from the present storm so the remainder of the remnant find their way home in the rapture before the coming Tribulation. May we all stop pretending for the faith for liberty is about to be vacated for the gallows of lawlessness.

The Boiling Pot Over Israel

Jeremiah 1

The word of the LORD came to me again: "What do you see?"

"I see a pot that is boiling," I answered. "It is tilting toward us from the north."

The LORD said to me, "From the north disaster will be poured out on all who live in the land. I am about to summon all the peoples of the northern kingdoms," declares the LORD.

"Their kings will come and set up their thrones

in the entrance of the gates of Jerusalem;

they will come against all her surrounding walls

and against all the towns of Judah.

I will pronounce my judgments on my people

because of their wickedness in forsaking me,

in burning incense to other gods

and in worshiping what their hands have made.

"Get yourself ready! Stand up and say to them whatever I command you.

Do not be terrified by them, or I will terrify you before them.

"Success is not final; failure is not fatal: it is the courage to continue that counts."
Winston S. Churchill

The forty-year ministry of the prophet Jeremiah was a tremendous display of faithfulness and courage in the face of great discouragement, opposition, with little results. The definition of Jeremiah was a reluctant prophet with "fire in his bones." He was very humble and very honest, almost to a fault. He was a perfect example of when God uses a person, He does not erase their personality. God always chose a man with a heart of passion and conviction.

A prophet in the Old Testament was someone who was used by God to communicate His message to the world. Prophets were also called "seers" because they could see as God gave them insight. As Jeremiah answered his calling, God asked him "What do you see?" The second thing that Jeremiah saw caused him to cry out with the warning that there was a boiling pot tilted toward

Jerusalem. This warned of the primary impending invasion of Jerusalem from Babylon, but the truth is they were already from their dark influence of chronic idolatry.

Israel had twisted herself like a harlot and had filled herself with lies of deception. She had listened to false prophets and not the prophets of God. Jeremiah then proclaimed to Israel an indictment from the Lord upon Jerusalem for their rabid betrayal and continual rebellion. This has been the solemn history of Israel being enslaved by the nations and their lust for the sensual. These evil spirits have appeared again moving from seduction to destruction. Israel now finds itself at the edge of the same twisted foes still trying to drive them "from the river to the sea.

Here are the verses with principled indictments over the boiling pot pouring out upon Israel.

They followed worthless idols and became worthless themselves.
Jerusalem abandoned the love, trust, fear, and the worship of God reaping the corruption of their national soul, In turn, they followed and were buffeted by the demonic.

What fault did your ancestors find in me that they strayed so far from Me?
God knew this was generational sin from unbelief ,extending from apathy and apostasy.

Because they have forsaken Me, they burned incense to other gods, and worshiped the works of their own hands.
The main reason for the coming judgment was Judah's chronic idolatry.

They shall come and each one set his throne at the entrance of the gates of Jerusalem.
Jeremiah prophetically saw the foreign kings dominating a subservient Jerusalem so the enemies of Jerusalem are here represented as conquering the whole land, assuming the reins of government, and laying the whole country under their laws being subjugated by their enemies. This will return in its fullness when the Antichrist brings Jerusalem's yearning for peace with a rebuilt temple that his image will be worshipped.

The Boiling Pot Over Our Nation

Luke 21

"Truly I tell you, this generation will certainly not pass away until all these things have happened. Heaven and earth will pass away, but my words will never pass away." Be careful, or your hearts will be weighed down with carousing, drunkenness and the anxieties of life, and that day will close on you suddenly like a trap. For it will come on all those who live on the face of the whole earth. Be always on the watch, and pray that you may be able to escape all that is about to happen, and that you may be able to stand before the Son of Man."

Israel set the pattern and the position of not only deviating from the faith, but she had completely rejected her Lord, shed her religious veneer, and becomes exactly like all the nations around her as a Harlot. Her adultery left naked and blind as we are now mocking her position among the nations. Their history was a tragic record of plunging into unfaithfulness and idol worship in betraying their God. The Lord sent one prophet after another to stand against their harlotry and affairs with the world. The history of Israel is a critical warning to us that those that do not learn from history are doomed to repeat it.

We discussed earlier the sifting of our nation and a merging uncivil war that has sifted the destiny of the nations scripturally. It is materializing as the perfect storm over the horizon. The boiling pot that once tilted over the nation of Israel is now tilting over the United States for the very same reasons. Its content of spiritual lawlessness, the same scarlet sin that invaded Jerusalem through Babylon is now pouring out upon our nation and all the nations. As former apostate Israel, we have abandoned the love and the worship of God as it corrupts our national soul. Generational sin ignited a chain reaction of worshipping the sensual idols from "selfism." The idols we now worship have possessed us of the nation as we follow sensual gratification by being infested by the demonized Mystery of Lawlessness. The spiritual undercurrent and the materialistic worship in our nation have brought us to a very dark place history.

Our nation is unrecognizable as we exchange the truth and the boundaries that have protected us since our inception for the Mystery of Lawlessness. As Israel has been Biblically portrayed as a Harlot for forsaking her God, our nation has quickly assumed the same path and identity. As Jeremiah witnessed the foreign kings enslaving a subservient Jerusalem, we have departed as blinded "dead men walking" in chains into a bottomless chamber of globalism with the elite "men of renown" ruling over us behind the scarlet curtain of harlotry.

If we do not begin to understand the fallacy of our ways and the spiritual seduction that is occurring, we will fulfill the carnal prophecies of Mystery Babylon. The collective description of this nation to be revealed in its time is right before our eyes. The idea of nuclear weapons would have been thought ludicrous until now. As technology and social media are grooming the planet for the final implosion, it will change the fabric of the globe and the eternal destiny of humanity. The mystery of the final Babylon will only be fulfilled at the coming judgment that has already invaded our shores. The dye has been cast and we are dimming by the moment. The Apostle Paul warned, "I urge you, in view of God's mercy, to offer your bodies as a living sacrifice, holy and pleasing to God, this is your true and proper worship. Worship is what you truly revere and value. The nations and the individual can only be sifted into two entities: the kingdom of God or the kingdom of darkness.

Closing the Book of Daniel

Daniel 12

"At that time Michael, the great prince who protects your people, will arise. There will be a time of distress such as has not happened from the beginning of nations until then. But at that time your people, everyone whose name is found written in the book, will be delivered. Multitudes who sleep in the dust of the earth will awake: some to everlasting life, others to shame and everlasting contempt. Those who are wise will shine like the brightness of the heavens, and those who lead many to righteousness, like the stars for ever and ever. But you, Daniel, roll up and seal the words of the scroll until the time of the end. Many will go here and there to increase knowledge."

The Book of Daniel is a beautiful tapestry that has been sealed through the ages until now. It ends with a prolific deliverance by the sifting blade of the Messiah taking place with Israel and the church. It speaks of the eternal resurrection of those written in the Book of Life. It is the separation of those who are wanderers in the darkness and "those who are wise that shine like the brightness of the heavens, leading many to righteousness."

Throughout the centuries, God has drawn people to be part of His Kingdom who have faced severe adversity. Daniel was one of these people who was counted as righteous. Daniel being removed from his homeland and taken to a foreign country in his teens must have been traumatic. Daniel's life, however, was to become an example for all of us. As the Book of Hebrews mentioned in the beginning "this is what the ancients were commended for." If we study Daniel, we will find the narrow path that leads to eternal life. Daniel lived his life in exile from a child and never experienced his homeland as he served the Lord in captivity his entire life which should encourage us today.

The name Daniel means "God is my judge." This declared his character and integrity as a man before God. His witness gained him favor with Babylon and their conquering empire, yet he refused to compromise his faith in God. Even under the intimidation of his kings, he remained steadfast in his commitment to God even to the threat of death. Daniel's life testified of the wisdom by the integrity of the Holy Spirit as he denied himself and followed the will of his Master.

Being a prophet of Israel, Daniel saw what the Apostle John envisioned concerning the time of trouble destined for Israel. These were twin revelations that revolve around the final prophecies of Israel, especially the crises with the Antichrist and the Abomination of Desolation during the Great Tribulation. Despite the terrors of his vision, deliverance was assured by Daniel. No matter how great the attack is against the Jewish people, God promises to preserve them. Daniel prophesied as he was moved by God through visions to happen throughout history. No vision was as important as his interpretation of the descending world empires leading to now. The vision is prolific even including the rise and fall of our nation and the final global ten-horned kingdom.

As Daniel, many young ones are now growing up in a post-Christian nation that is daily being stripped of its eternal heritage. Israel set the pattern for invasion from weakness by crumbling from within through apostasy. Our Christian heritage has been diluted from generational apathy and a thirst for idolatry. It is fascinating that Daniel even prophesied the explosion of knowledge and technology at the final sifting that devours those trampled in the final Day of Evil. The fall of our nation has fallen upon our children. Their cries of anger and sedition are proceeding from abandonment as we have abandoned our faith in God. As Daniel and his brethren, they will overcome by their testimony.

As Daniel warned, "Multitudes who sleep in the dust of the earth will awaken: some to everlasting life, others to shame and everlasting contempt." Do we represent a beacon of love as we once did, or do we testify to the "great lie" that our god is our senses and our choice? is not just a sifting taking place between who will face judgment concerning faithfulness, but also who will be removed at the rapture. We seem to have all of the answers, but we need to remember the questions.

Daniel was told to go his way until the end. Though his mind was filled with exciting and frightening prophetic visions, it would have been easy for those things to become a distraction instead of a blessing. God had a mission that He wanted Daniel to complete, and Daniel needed to remain focused. This is the blueprint for us to trust in God, fearing only Him. It is now the time for the scroll from Daniel to be unsealed.

Where is the Promise of His Coming?

2 Peter 3

Above all, you must understand that in the last days scoffers will come, scoffing and following their own evil desires. They will say, "Where is this 'coming' he promised? Ever since our ancestors died, everything goes on as it has since the beginning of creation." But they deliberately forget that long ago by God's word the heavens came into being and the earth was formed out of water and by water. By these waters also the world of that time was deluged and destroyed. By the same word the present heavens and earth are reserved for fire, being kept for the day of judgment and destruction of the ungodly. But do not forget this one thing, dear friends: With the Lord a day is like a thousand years, and a thousand years are like a day. The Lord is not slow in keeping his promise, as some understand slowness. Instead, he is patient with you, not wanting anyone to perish, but everyone to come to repentance.

"Every time a blasphemer opens his mouth to deny the truth of revelation, he will help to confirm us in our conviction of the very truth which he denies. The Holy Ghost told us, by the pen of Peter, that it would be so; and now we see how truly he wrote." Charles Spurgeon

As with Daniel's remnant, the sifting blade of the Messiah is cleansing and separating the faithful from the unbelieving apostates. Today's religious hypocrites wander in the darkness questioning God and his chosen, with lies and excuses to justify their selfish existence. The greatest indictment of God deriving from their rebellion was that God never keeps His promises and he is a deserter. The truth is that they are the deserters.

The "scoffers" in Peter's day, were unrepentant mockers ignoring that His coming will be like a thief in the night. They did not watch for Him; they just drown in their skepticism and heartlessness. These "scoffers" did not only have an intellectual problem with God and His word, They also had a distinct moral problem, wanting to reject the Lordship of Jesus Christ over their lives. The scoffers take hostage the mercy and longsuffering of God, insisting that because they have never seen a widespread judgment of God, that there will never be one. But they willfully forget God's creation and the judgment God poured out on the earth in the days of Noah.

Peter saw right through their excessive rioting that was destroying the others around them. The Apostle Peter was "crazy as a fox" as he responded with a peculiar example of what repentance and baptism entails. He testified that the generation of Noah was birthed and judged through the same deep water of its creation as he chose in its time. The living Word of the Messiah which brings both life and judgement will be pronounced in His time once again. The truth is that God will keep His promise, and without delay according to His timing. Any perceived is due to the longsuffering of God, who allows man as much time as possible to repent. Peter tells us that the Lord's promises are not slow, as the scoffers protested. As He is patiently waiting, He is not wanting anyone to perish, but His patience is about to run out.

Seeing Through the Glass Darkly

1 Corinthians 13

Love never fails. But where there are prophecies, they will cease; where there are tongues, they will be stilled; where there is knowledge, it will pass away. For we know in part and we prophesy in part, [10] but when completeness comes, what is in part disappears. When I was a child, I talked like a child, I thought like a child, I reasoned like a child. When I became a man, I put the ways of childhood behind me. For now, we see only a reflection as in a mirror; then we shall see face to face. Now I know in part; then I shall know fully, even as I am fully known. And now these three remain: faith, hope and love. But the greatest of these is love.

Is there still time for us to repent, or is it already too late? Before we continue, a word to those who do not believe we have time to repent, who believe that God must judge us because of what we already have done, and not done. Such beliefs are not biblical, and those who hold them are themselves enjoined to repent. Eric Metaxas

Corinth was one of the great cities of the ancient world, and a community that was outwardly prosperous, busy, and thriving. It had a deserved reputation for the reckless pursuit of pleasure. The Corinthian people were world renown for drunkenness, wild partying and loose sexual morals. The term "Korinthiazomai" was well known in the Roman Empire and it literally meant "to live like a Corinthian." It had a hedonistic heart that became apparent in the church. Corinth was famous for producing some of the best bronze mirrors, but at their best, they couldn't give a clear vision, but a darkened perception. The Corinthian church appeared to be a "rich" church, but as the church in Laodicea, "they were poor, naked, and blind." Things were happening in the church that were unspeakable, even to the city around them. "The failure on the part of the Church was the measure in which she has allowed herself to be influenced by the spirit of the age.

Paul confessed "when he became a man, he put the ways of childhood behind him. This was an indictment to convict an immature church of being a nominal expression of the world surrounding it. He expressed that childish things are appropriate for children, and the gifts of the Holy Spirit were appropriate for the present time, but would not be appropriate forever. Paul was not trying to say that if we are spiritually mature, we will not need spiritual gifts. But he does say that if we are spiritually mature, we will not idolize them at the expense of love. The gifts of the Holy Spirit are necessary and appropriate for this present age, when we are not yet fully mature, and we only know in part. There will come a day when the gifts are unnecessary, but that day has not come yet.

Today, I am not quite sure which is the most blind or deaf; our nation or the nominal church. The silence in the church is deafening while our nation rages in "selfism." I do know that Jesus spoke these words concerning the very hour of trial that is upon us. "Because of the increase of wickedness, the love of most will grow cold, but the one who stands firm to the end will be saved." Satan has set the final gauntlet within his worldwide web and we all must choose to inflame "agape love" or death by consenting.

The Apostle Paul was very tough on the church in Corinth for very good reasons. The first rebuke was their childish attitude of being seduced as Eve from a "simple and pure devotion to Christ." They loved their gifts more than the Giver. They had forgotten the cornerstone that "agape love" never changes or fades. It is a self-giving love that gives without demanding or expecting repayment. Paul expressed that even if you give your body to be burned, apart from love, it has no profit.

I must ask how complicit today is the nominal church by hiding behind their four walls ignoring the flames devouring this generation? Witnessing the fall of our last two generations from the trenches has infuriated me, but it has also taught me how critical it is about who and what we follow. The sins of the fathers have been visited upon their children along with the violence from the gang leaders replacing them. They are forced to follow those who have never grown up, but just have gotten older. They hate what the system has become and the patent lies are screaming at them from the abyss of delusion. The glass doesn't get any darker than this.

Except for Jesus Christ, there is no one that exemplified Israel and the church more than the Apostle Paul. He did not feel worthy of the call to be an apostle, yet his volatile past was a testament of shame leading to the glory of God in his future. The Book of Acts testified of his violent mission to destroy the church where the Lord blinded him so he could see. This is why he called himself "the very least of all the saints" for a very valid reason.

Despite his past, Paul truly understood his deep failure, but he clearly realized he had been specifically sent by God on the road to Damascus. He did not ask for his calling, but received it through receiving salvation by grace through faith. Paul wonderfully described his journey by, "forgetting what is behind and straining toward what is ahead, I press on toward the goal to win the prize for which God has called me heavenward in Christ Jesus."

Paul matured to the point that he challenged the church by boldly stating, "Love never fails. But whether there are prophecies, they will fail; whether there are tongues, they will cease; whether there is knowledge, it will vanish away." A critical question to ask yourself is "where have you been and where are you going?"

God's ways are far beyond our carnal understanding. His riches are far beyond our human ability to search or examine. Paul's future witness would emphasize that fact that his mission would end his life. He could not and would not have chosen his narrow path. Yet, God had a deeper purpose in calling Paul, which changed countless lives as he eventually expressed his confidence in boldly declaring, "follow me."

As with the conversion from Saul to Paul, I have received a doctorate from the school of hard knocks from my own devices. Yet, I have to say, there is a precious revelation that helped radically change my Christian life. It was to learn to live from acceptance, not for acceptance. It helped give me the courage of my convictions from being lost as my eternal compass spun in the wrong direction. As Paul, I could not and would not have chosen this narrow path. Yet, our lives must be filled with suffering passion for love and the truth to resist the dark regime of the enemy.

Don't Lose Heart

They came to John and said to him, "Rabbi, that man who was with you on the other side of the Jordan, the one you testified about, look, he is baptizing, and everyone is going to him."

To this John replied, "A person can receive only what is given them from heaven. ²You yourselves can testify that I said, 'I am not the Messiah but am sent ahead of him.' The bride belongs to the bridegroom. The friend who attends the bridegroom waits and listens for him, and is full of joy when he hears the bridegroom's voice. That joy is mine, and it is now complete. He must become greater; I must become less."

    The above verses are an incredible prophetic blueprint from John the Baptist, the greatest and final prophet. John's mission was simply repentance through baptism. From the beginning of his mission, John saw right through the religious veneer of the pharisees and their parade of ritual. He reviled them by saying, "You brood of vipers! Who warned you to flee from the coming wrath? Produce fruit in keeping with repentance." They were barren because they loved the attention more than the truth. Secondly, John understood that he was not the light, but like us, he came only to be a witness to the light.

If the meaning of baptism can be summarized in one word, that would be "reidentification." It is a spiritual burial and the process of cleansing to an identification to the image of the Messiah. When John declared that "joy is mine, and it is now complete. He must become greater; and I must become less." John's entrance to heaven had eventually arrived from a blade where he was beheaded for the most despicable reason. As the disciples, "he learned to lose his life to find it."

At this lowest point in his life, John sent two of his disciples to ask Jesus the question, "Are you the one to come after me or shall we wait for another?" This rhetorical question contained its own answer. As John was beyond discouraged, he felt that Jesus had forgotten and forsaken him as he surely felt a sense of betrayal. He misunderstood that his decrease was happening and he was not getting released from prison, but released to heaven. Just like us, it was hard for John to let go. Jesus reminded him that he had plowed faithfully for another to reap.

There is great assurance by the witness of John when he stumbled in his circumstances. Thank God for the hope we see in his doubt that we are not alone, it is about what is in front of us. It was not evidence of John's destiny; it was proof he had not yet arrived. It is an exposure of every one of us at one point or another. The most important lesson from this is when we have fallen short, He is waiting with His grace and reassurance to identify us.

When Jesus responded to John, He said, "Go back and report to John what you have seen and heard" with His reassurance and mercy that He had this. That is His word for you "to not fear. I have you." Jesus revives us through repenting every day, every hour, and every second. It is easy but dangerous to lose heart. In the ancient world, this phrase translated lose heart was used for the kind of fear and weariness a woman experiences during labor before delivery. The pharisees believed in the wrath to come; the difference was who were the targets of that judgment. They conceived of the judgment was concerning the gentiles, never realizing that it was concerning the godless in Israel. This is the recurring dilemma with the nominal church. John knowing that Christ must increase as he must decrease is a distinct pattern for us to parallel with being a wise virgin.

Remember Our Precious Messiah

Therefore, we do not lose heart. Though outwardly we are wasting away, yet inwardly we are being renewed day by day. For our light and momentary troubles are achieving for us an eternal glory that far outweighs them all. So, we fix our eyes not on what is seen, but on what is unseen, since what is seen is temporary, but what is unseen is eternal.

We share with Israel the blessed eternal hope, and promise of the Messiah. Isaiah promised that God would send Israel the light and joy through the birth of a child who would break the "yoke of their burden." Paul said, "My dear children, for whom I am again in the pains of childbirth until Christ is formed in you." The time for Israel has arrived as the water of Israel's birth has broken for their redemption. The Messiah will soon complete them.

Our completion will be birthed if we continually pick up our cross and begin to fear the Lord again. The Messianic promises are always based upon two stages; the remedy from sin and the power of deliverance. The two pieces of the cross speaks to the same but it reveals practical relationship. The vertical beam reveals our heavenly purpose cleansed by the precious blood as the horizontal reveals our earthly mission to others by relating the cross to our life to others. Without repentance and obedience, our life is powerless.

There is a peculiar parable for the transforming mystery of godliness from the very peculiar place of the weapon of mass destruction. The process for an atomic bomb is incredibly complex for this very simple purpose; to create an implosion. Nuclear fission produces energy through a fracture of atoms that create this implosion. The basic idea is to take an atom like uranium, bombard it with neutrons so that the atoms each absorb an extra neutron, causing them to become an unstable isotope that is prone to undergo a nuclear implosion. The degradation becomes a new atom, causing an immeasurable explosion of energy. This is the pattern that is set in the hearts of the redeemed.

We have to realize the deeper reality of Christ's question, "What good is it for someone to gain the whole world, yet forfeit their soul?" It is proven that not one prophetic word will fall to the ground. So, be encouraged that your labor in Christ is not in vain. The Apostle Paul continually related the beautiful references to struggling from sifting and being transforming into the image of our Lord Jesus Christ. One of the most important revelations was "for the message of the cross is foolishness to those who are perishing, but to us who are being saved, it is the power of God.

The second most difficult task that I ever did was building my log home in Colorado. In prayer one morning, I was inspired to do something that a pastor would catch a lot of grief for doing. I went down to Denver and had a tattoo on my forearm of the cross with the scripture ending the Book of Galatians. Paul said, "From now on I let no one trouble me, for I bear on my body that testify to His ownership of me."

This came from Paul again having to rescue the innocent from the "wolves in sheep's clothing," in the battle for gullible lambs. He was referring to the legalistic Christians among the Galatians and wrote frankly about their motive to make a good showing in the flesh. They worked to bring the Galatian Christians from a Gentile background under circumcision because it would be a good showing for them, but a good showing in the flesh. We must be "wise as a serpent but harmless as a dove.

The heart and soul of this book is to reiterate the promise and process from the sifting blade of our Messiah. I am saying this from the bottom of my heart. You deeply matter to God and you matter to me, but if we do not truly find our knees we will perish. There is a shaking and sifting in our nation and our hearts that will mark the eternal future. This specific book is the hardest thing I have ever done because it has been birthed from having blood up to my elbows from younger tormented souls. I leave you with the hope of your calling.

Revelation 22
"Look, I am coming soon! My reward is with me, and I will give to each person according to what they have done. I am the Alpha and the Omega, the First and the Last, the Beginning and the End. "Blessed are those who wash their robes, that they may have the right to the tree of life and may go through the gates into the city. 15 Outside are the dogs, those who practice magic arts, the sexually immoral, the murderers, the idolaters and everyone who loves and practices falsehood.

The Second Book of the Trilogy

Available
on Amazon Books

In the Valley of Decision is the second book of this spiritual trilogy. The ferocious prophetic whirlwind of the Mystery of Lawlessness spiraling through the Sixties" has now created the perfect storm leading into the Valley of Decision in Megiddo. We are experiencing every prophetic sign from Jesus Christ's with the "Beginning of Sorrows." The Sixties became a collage of personal and cultural exploits, most that turned the heart of man ice cold toward God and inward into re-birth of "selfism." It ushered in the Mystery of Lawlessness that the Apostle Paul warned would complete the fatal Way of Cain. With the journey to the moon, the lancing of racial tensions, the challenge of stagnant politics and apostate religion, seeded the great deception.

Coming Soon on Amazon Books

The Harlot's Cup **at the Twilights Last Gleaming**
This book is not for the weak at heart. It is a serious look at the present spiritual battle with the Prince of this World and how is dispensing the Great Apostasy and the Mystery of Lawless through the cup of the Harlot that would deceive the very elect of God if it were possible. The Harlot's Cup exposes the global reset and where our nation fits in Biblical prophecy. It reveals the Mystical Harlot of Babylon, her rise and demise in the final hour and the contents of sorcery from her mystical cup of delusion.